Daoist

Cultivation

XII

Vitaly Filbert

Daoist Cultivation

The Daoist Classic

The Secret of the Golden Flower

Translation and Commentary

by Vitaly Filbert

Book 12

2023

Daoist Cultivation Press

Los Angeles, CA, USA

This book is not intended to replace a Teacher and provides general information on the topics discussed. The author and publisher disclaim any liability or loss, personal or other, as a result of the information or content in this book. The information in this book is for educational purposes only.

Contents

Introduction

"The Secret of the Golden Flower" was one of the first spiritual texts I read. I was 15 years old and still in high school when one of my friends gave me a book containing a collection of traditional texts of Buddhism and Daoism. "The Secret of the Golden Flower" was one of them, and this particular text was translated by Richard Wilhelm. In addition to the "Golden Flower," there was "Dao De Jing" by Lao Zi, some instructions from the ancient Masters of Chan Buddhism, traditional texts of the Pure Land and Tiantai Buddhist schools, and some others. In those days, this book was a great treasure to me. When I read it for the first time, I did not understand anything, but I sensed in it a profound wisdom, some kind of mysterious connection with Buddhism and Daoism, especially with Daoism. After that, I read it over and over again, it was a huge number of times. I even took this book to school and kept reading it in class, despite the warnings of teachers. Eventually, I began to understand some things and tried to follow some of the instructions from that book. This is how my encounter with this text happened. And that book was just the beginning, laying the foundation for a long journey.

As I already mentioned, "The Secret of the Golden Flower" in that book was a translation by Richard Wilhelm with commentaries by psychologist C. G. Jung. Many years later, I found out that it was a poor translation, containing misleading information and misinterpreting many parts of the text. Since C. G. Jung's commentaries are based on this translation, there is no sense in commenting on it. In addition, the last five chapters, 9-13, have not been translated at all. But nevertheless, it was from him that I learned about this scripture.

There is one more well-known translation by Thomas Cleary, but he didn't use traditional Daoist terms in his translation. For instance, instead of Yang and Yin, he used "positive energy" or "positivity" and "negative energy" or "negativity." But, frankly, Yin and Yang are special terms that include deeper meanings than just "negativity" or "positivity." That is why in my translation, I have left all the special terms as they are. Also, some fragments of the text were not translated by Thomas Cleary.

The text contains quotes from different sources, and I denote from which particular sources they were taken. On top of that, there are many Buddhist ideas and terms in the text, such as "Zhi Guan," which is the method of the Tiantai school of Mahayana Buddhism. I was familiar with the Zhi Guan method since high school, and later studied it more deeply. The text also includes some Confucian thoughts.

The text is accompanied by many of my commentaries, in which I explain difficult-to-understand terms, fragments of the text, or why I translated certain pieces in one way or another.

The full title of the text in Chinese 吕祖先天一气太乙金华宗旨 or "Main Principles of the Pre-Celestial One Qi of the Golden Flower of the Great Unity by Patriarch Lu (Dòngbīn)." It later becomes shorter 太乙金华宗旨 - tàiyǐ jīnhuá zōngzhǐ, which means "Main Principles of the Golden Flower of the Great Unity." Even though "The Secret of the Golden Flower" is not a very accurate translation, I still used it because that's the better-known title among Western practitioners.

Although the text is written in Lu Dongbin's name, some Daoists believe that the text was written by one of his students, Wang Chongyang (王重阳).

Chapter 1

Heart-Mind of Heaven

4

Naturalness is called the Dao-Way.

The Dao-Way has no name and no form.

It is the Original Nature - Xing, it is the Original Spirit-Shen.

The Original Nature - Xing and Vitality-Ming cannot be seen, but they rely on the Light of Heaven;

The Light of Heaven cannot be seen, but it relays on eyes.

Since ancient times, Immortals and True People transmitted (this knowledge) from mouth to mouth, from one (disciple) to another.

Tai Shang* suddenly manifested itself, and Donghua** transmitted (knowledge of the Way) further to the ancestors-founders of the Southern and Northern Schools. Quanzhen*** School began to flourish.

---

* 太上 - Tai Shang is a title that can be translated as "Great Higher," "Great Supreme," or "Uppermost."

** Means Dong Hua Di Jun, he is the Emperor of Heaven, one of the Daoist deities born from nothingness.

*** Quanzhen - 全真- is one of the most famous Northern Schools founded by Wang Chongyang (王重阳). Quanzhen can be translated as "Complete Truth," "Complete Perfection," or "Complete True-Reality."

"Flourish" (in the sense that Teaching) is spread among many people and has many followers, but at the same time, it led to a weak (and incomplete) transmission of knowledge (between students) to the present day.

That which extremely grows up inevitably falls down*.

* This line can also be translated as "What is too widespread is greatly distorted."

When the extreme is reached, the reverse appears.

In ancient times, there was a founder-ancestor of the School of Pure Clarity, Master Xu**

** This is about Master Xu Xun - 许逊 - (239-374) also known as Xu Jingyang. He was a student of Master Wu Meng (吴猛) and the founder of the School of Jìng Míng Pài (净明派) or the School of Pure Clarity. Xu

6

Xun, Zhang Daoling (张道陵), Ge Xuan (葛玄), and Sa Shoujian (萨守坚) are also known as the Four Heavenly Masters (天师) of Daoism.

This line in the original text is 故蒙净明许祖, where 故 means "ancient times, therefore." 蒙 means "to receive (a favor), cover, overspread, ignorance, illiteracy," 净明 means "Pure Clarity," 许祖 means "master/ancestor/founder Xu."

He expressed compassion and mercy in order to save all beings and established the Teaching of Transmission Intention-Essence Outside of Doctrine to meet and guide (people with) high skills.

It is hard to meet those who heard about it, but those who accepted it organized the Teaching assembly.

Everyone should pay tribute to the painstaking efforts of the heart-mind of founder-ancestor Master Xu.

Establishing ethical relations in everyday life, in any activity, is necessary, and this is a firm foothold.

Only then will you be able to study the True-Reality and comprehend the Original Nature - Xing.

Today I have the honor to be your Teacher and guide you.

First, I will clarify the main meaning of the text "Tai Yi Jin Hua"*, then I will explain it in detail.

* 太乙金华 - Tai Yi Jin Hua - literally means "Golden Flower of Great Unity."

Great Unity points to the Highest-Supreme.

There are many alchemical secret methods, but they all use Being to achieve Non-Doing, and there is no way to get into it directly.

Therefore, the main idea-essence that I transmit brings you to work with the Original Nature - Xing, without focusing on secondary methods**.

That is why it is marvelous.

** It does not mean that secondary methods are wrong, it means that they work more with the Essence-Jing and Energy-Qi and less with the Original Nature - Xing. For a solid foundation, it is necessary to start with secondary methods, and they will help you to achieve a healthy body and mind, balance Yin and Yang, etc., much faster because they were created for these purposes. So, technically, these are Ming Gong methods.

8

But be sure to also keep in mind the Xing Gong work during Ming Gong; in this case, you can naturally follow the dual Cultivation of Xing and Ming and achieve the best results. If you do not prepare your body and mind with secondary methods, then you will not be able to follow the main methods because your body will be unhealthy, and your heart-mind will not be purified. And your work will not be completed because it requires a solid foundation which should be built by Ming Gong techniques.

That is why this text by Lu Dongbin is not for beginners.

Golden Flower is the Light.

What color is the Light?

It (Light) is a symbol of the Golden Flower, and this Light is hidden within.

This is the True Original Qi-Energy of Precelestial Great Unity.

That is why there is a saying, "The Lead of Water region has only one place/location*."

* See trigram Water.

Here the character 位 - wèi - was translated as place/location, but in some sources, instead of 位 - wèi, the character 味 is put, which has the same pronunciation - "wèi," but in this case, it translates as "taste." In my translation, I chose the first wèi - 位 - because it makes more sense in this case because of the trigram of Water, which is obviously the "Water region," with one solid line inside, which indicates the Lead.

More information about Lead and Mercury, Water and Fire, Dragon and Tiger, etc., you can find in "Chapters on Awakening to the True Reality" (悟真篇) by Daoist Master Zhang Boduan (张伯端). It was translated in Book 6.

Light Return Mastery is maintained by using reverse flow and focus on the Heart-Mind of Heaven.

The Heart-Mind of Heaven is located between the Sun and the Moon*.

* Sun and Moon mean eyes

Huángtíng Jīng* says, "In the field of the square inch of the house of the square foot**, life can be regulated."

* Huángtíng Jīng (黄庭经) or "Treatise of the Yellow Court" is one of the Daoist texts about Cultivation, and it is believed that Wei Huacun was the author. Wei Huacun (魏华存) lived 252–334, was a practitioner of the Celestial Master School (天师道 - Tian Shi Dao) and the founder of Shang Qing School (上清派) or School of Highest Clarity. Because the school was centered on Mount Mao (茅山), it is also known as the Maoshan School.

** This saying indicates the location of the upper Dantian.

The house of the square foot is the face.

The field of the square inch is on the face.

What could it be if not the Heart-Mind of Heaven?

In the center of the square inch, there is wonderful scenery, the uncanny Cinnabar Palace of the Jade Capital, where the Spirit-Shen of Utmost Emptiness and Ultimate Spirituality dwells.

The Confucians call it the Center of Emptiness.

The Buddhists say - The Spiritual Platform.**

The Daoists - the Founders-Ancestors Land, the Yellow Court, the Mysterious Gate, or the Precelestial Opening/Orifice.

** 灵台 - língtái - the place where the spirit resides

The Heart-Mind of Heaven is like the dwelling place and the Light is the master (of the house).

Therefore once you Return the Light, then the Qi-Energy of the whole body is raised to the royal court*.

* Means to the upper Dantian

Just like the Sage Emperor established his capital, a dynasty, and affirmed the highest truth/rules.

Tribute will be given by all states.**

** 玉帛 - yùbó - jade objects and silk fabrics used as state gifts.

Just like a shrewd master, to whom servants and maids naturally obey orders and perform their duties.

All you have to do is just Return the Light.

This is the unexcelled supreme truth.

The Light is easy to move but difficult to stabilize-condense.

If you keep Returning (the Light) for a long time, it will be (eventually) condensed and naturally form the True Body*.

* True Body -法身 (Fǎshēn) - is a Buddhist term for the Sanskrit word Dharmakaya. It can also be translated as Essential Body and is a part of the trikaya doctrine, which literally means "three bodies" or "three personalities." According to this doctrine, Buddha has three bodies: Dharmakaya or Essential Body, Sambhogakāya - 報身 - Bao Shen - or Bliss Body, and Nirmāṇakāya - 應身 - Ying Shen - or Transformation Body.

Eventually, you will be able to keep condensed Spirit-Shen over the Nine Worlds of Heavens**.

That is why, in Xīnyìn Jīng, *** said: "In silence, be privately invited to a meeting with the Emperor of Heaven; After one period of time of twelve years, you will ascend in one moment."****.

** In general, it means that you will transcend all the things and worlds-realms in Being and Non-Being.

The original text uses the characters 九霄 - jiǔxiāo - Nine Worlds of Heavens. According to Daoist cosmology, there are Nine Worlds of Heaven. It doesn't really matter if it's true or not. Sometimes in ancient times, some sections of cosmology were created simply for the convenience of explaining a particular phenomenon. They are just symbols pointing to something and different manifestations of Higher Truth, Supreme, Dao, or whatever name you prefer. It's like a finger that points to the moon; it's not the finger that matters, but the moon.

*** 心印经 - Xīnyìn jīng (Heart Seal scripture), also known as 高上玉皇心印妙经 Gaoshang Yuhuang Xinyin Miao Jing. It was written before the Southern Song Dynasty (1127–1279), most likely from the end of the Tang Dynasty and the Five Dynasties (907-960) to the end of the Northern Song Dynasty (960-1127). This scripture was widely popular and it became one of the Quanzhen classics.

**** In this text, this line is 默朝飞升, but in Xīnyìn jīng, it is actually four characters longer - 默朝上帝 一纪飞升. I translated a line from Xīnyìn text.

"A period of twelve years" (一纪) refers to the stages of "Three years of feeding" and "Facing the wall for nine years." You can find information about these stages in Book 7.

"Invited to a meeting with the Emperor of Heaven" indicates a specific work with upper dantian.

To implement the main purpose-essence, you do not need to look for other methods;

Just keep this pure and perfect idea-intention.

Léngyán Jīng* says:

"If you can keep pure and perfect idea-intention, you can ascend and be born in Heaven"**.

It refers not to the blue Sky-Heaven but to the body born in the palace of (trigram) Qian***.

Over time, you will naturally have a body besides the body you already have.

* Léngyán Jīng (楞严经) is a Surangama Sutra. This is a Mahayana Buddhist guidebook and is especially important for Zen/Chan Buddhism. Śūraṅgama means "heroic valor," "heroic progress," or "heroic march" in Sanskrit.

** This line is taken from the eighth scroll of Léngyán Jīng/Surangama Sutra.

*** Qian (乾) is one of the eight trigrams, and it symbolizes Heaven. In the human body, it is the head.

The Golden Flower is the Golden Elixir.

The Spirit is enlightened and transformed in accordance with the heart-mind of each person.

This is the Marvelous secret method;

Although it does not have a single drop of difference, it is still very flexible.

It all depends on your intelligence, brightness, and your ability to remain in deep Stillness and Quietness.

That is why not very smart people cannot use/follow it, and people who cannot remain in deep Stillness and Quietness will not be able to hold it.

Chapter 2

Original Spirit and Conscious Spirit

Compared to Heaven and Earth, people are like mayflies.

Compared to Great Dao, Heaven and Earth are like bubbles on water.

Only the True Original Nature - Xing of Original Spirit-Shen transcends anything and everything.

Even Essence-Jing and Energy-Qi follow Heaven and Earth and degenerate/decay.

Fortunately, there is the Original Spirit-Shen, which is Wuji*;

The Heaven and the Earth are born from there.

* Wuji (无极) means "limitless, infinite," the state before the existence of Heaven and Earth. This is a very old concept, and Lao Zi mentions Wuji in Dao De Jing: "Being a model for the world, And the constant Virtue-De will be flawless, (you can) Returning to the state of Limitless-Wuji." Dao De Jing is translated in Book 8.

Those who study the Path can guard and protect Original Spirit-Shen.

They can transcend Yin and Yang* and not be in the Three Realms**.

* Means a world of duality.

** Three Realms (三界) are also discussed in Wang Chongyang's Fifteen Discourses Establishing the Teaching: "The Realm of Desires, the Realm of Forms, and the Realm of Formlessness are the Three Realms." The text was translated and explained in Book 9.

You only need to comprehend your Original Nature - Xing, which is also called "to See your Original/True Face."

When ordinary people are incarnate, then their Original Spirit-Shen dwells in a square inch (between the eyes), and the Conscious Spirit lives in the heart.

The heart of flesh and blood, shaped like a large peach, covered by the lungs, supported by the liver, and served by the large and small intestines.

If you do not eat for one day, it feels very uncomfortable.

If it hears something terrifying, it throbs;

If it hears something angry, it suffocates;

If it sees death, it becomes sad;

If it sees something beautiful, it is dazzled.

But the Heart-Mind of Heaven on the top of your head, when did it even move a little!?

If you want to ask: Can the Heart-Mind of Heaven not move?

The answer is: How can the True Intention in a square inch move!?

If it moves, it is not good, but at the same time, it can be exceptionally marvelous.

When it moves, ordinary people die, which is why it is not good.

It can be exceptionally marvelous when the Light condenses into the True Body and is gradually filled with the innermost spirituality, and then it intends to move.

This is a secret that has not been transmitted through the ages.

The conscious heart-mind is like an imperious and despotic general protecting his lands;

He (tries) to intimidate higher authority but only shows his weakness and ignorance and only evades the observance of the law.

Over time, he can even compromise the higher authority and seize power.

But if you condense and protect the Original Palace, it will be like a wise ruler is in charge.

With two eyes, bring back the Light;

It is like having ministers who help you with all their hearts.

As a result, the internal governance will be clear and regulated, and all treacherous rebels and traitors will naturally switch sides and beg for mercy.

The Way of Elixir uses Essence-Jing as Water, Spirit-Shen as Fire, and Intention as Earth.

These three are the highest treasures.

What is Water of Essence-Jing?

It is the Precelestial True One Qi-Energy.

The Fire of Spirit-Shen is the Light.

The Intention of Earth is the Heart-Mind of Heaven in the Central Palace.

Use the Fire of Spirit-Shen as a function of influence, the Intention of Earth as a body-substance, and the Water of Essence-Jing as a foundation.

The body of the incarnation of an ordinary person depends on thoughts*.

* That is why Daoism insists on starting Cultivation from the Purification of the heart-mind, De-Virtue Cultivation, etc. It will help you to avoid many obstacles in the future, choose the right decision in difficult life situations, distinguish lies from the truth, and have many other benefits.

The body is not just the seven feet tall physical body, there are Po-Souls** within it.

Po-Souls rely on the Conscious (Spirit) and use it, and the Conscious (Spirit) rely on Po-Souls at birth.

** Po-Souls (魄) correspond to the Yin side of Shi Shen (Conscious Spirit), i.e., which contributes to the attraction of us to the Earth. It is they who attract us to indulge base desires and passions. This is the so-called animal primitive part of us. They occupy 7 of 10 parts of the Conscious Spirit.

You can find more information about Shi Shen (Conscious Spirit), Yuan Shen (Original Spirit), Po-Souls and Hun-Souls in Book 1.

Po-Souls are Yin and body-substance of Conscious (Spirit).

If Conscious (Spirit) is not broken-interrupted, Po-Souls, due to transformations, endlessly change the form-body from life to life, from generation to generation.

Also, there are Hun-Souls,* this is the place where your mind-intelligence is hidden.

* Hun-Souls (魂) correspond to the Yang side of Shi Shen, and this is the intelligent, spiritual part of the Conscious Spirit. Hun Souls are the light and intellectual side of our Spirit of Recognition, but they occupy only three parts out of ten.

During the day, the Hun-Souls reside in the eyes and dwell in the liver at night.

When they are in the eyes, people can see;

When they dwell in the liver, people can dream.

Dreams are the wanderings of the Spirit-Shen through nine Heavens and the nine Lands;

You can go around everything in an instant.

If, after waking up, you are in a gloomy and dull state, it means that you have been captured-restrained by the form-body, which is fettered by the Po-Souls.

Therefore, by Returning the Light, you can Refine-Cultivate the Hun-Souls, to guard-protect the Spirit-Shen, control the Po-Souls, and to break-interrupt the (bad influence of) consciousness.

The ancients method of transcending the world of life and death is refining the Yin** defilements and returning to the pure Yang***

** Means all kinds of ignorance and delusion.

*** The original text uses the character 乾 (Qián), which

Qian (Heaven)

24

means the trigram of Heaven consisting of three solid Yang lines.

In fact, it is simply the elimination of the Po-Souls in order to make the Hun-Souls complete and perfect.

Returning the Light is the secret of dissolving-eliminating of Yin in order to control the Po-Souls.

Although, there is no method to restore Qian*, only the secret of Returning the Light.

* 乾 - Qian or the trigram of Heaven, in other words, pure Yang.

The Light is (trigram) Qian; Return is restoration.

Only by following this method can you naturally refill the Water of Essence-Jing, ignite the Fire of Spirit-Shen, and condense-crystallize the Intention of Earth.

Then the Spiritual Embryo will be formed.

A dung beetle rolls the ball, and life is born inside** this ball***, which is a pure result of concentrated-focused Spirit-Shen.

** In these species, males take a lump of excrement from a dung heap, form a ball, and roll it away. If a female likes what she sees, she may hop on the dung ball and ride on it while the male pushes his prize to the perfect spot. Once in a good location, the pair digs a dung ball into the soft soil, mates, and lays an egg in it.

*** 丸 - wán - general meaning for a small round object. Also, it is a hint of a correlation with Níwán (泥丸), which is the Palace of Muddy/Clay Pellet and is one of the Nine Palaces in the head and it occupies the central position among the Nine Palaces of the head. Niwan Palace is the part where Yuan Shen (元神) lives and the reason why we are Returning the Light.

If life can be born inside a ball of manure and shed its shell, then why cannot the dwelling place of the Heart-Mind of Heaven also be able to create the (True) Body by concentrated-condensed Spirit-Shen?

When the One Spiritual True Original Nature is in the Palace of Qian-Heaven, it divides into Hun-Souls and Po-Souls.

The Hun-Souls are located in the Heart-Mind of Heaven; they are Yang, bright and clear.

Their source is the Great Emptiness, which is also the Original Beginning.

The Po-Souls are Yin, they are addicted to turbid Qi-Energy and are attached to worldly desires of the ordinary heart-mind.

The Hun-Souls like life, but the Po-Souls look toward death.

Lust, temper, and all other bad habits are controlled by Po-Souls, which are also the Conscious Spirit-Shen*.

* Since they occupy 7 out of 10 parts of the Conscious Spirit, it is much easier to degrade than develop spiritually.

After death, it feeds on blood; during life - great suffering.

Yin returns to Yin**.

Things of one kind come together.

** Some people think that Yin and Yang forces attract each other, but it is incorrect. Yin and Yang are opposite forces, like fire and water. We have here a similarity-attraction effect, which was also explained by Daoist Master Zhang Boduan (張伯端) in his book Wuzhen Pian: "If the bamboo is cracked, you need to use bamboo to repair it; If you want to hatch a chicken, you need an egg. If things are not of the same kind, your efforts are useless." This text is translated in Book 6.

Explanations of the relationship between Yin and Yand are given in Book 1.

If anyone who studies (the Dao-Way) can refine-purify all the Yin of the Po-Souls, he will reach the pure Yang.

Chapter 3

Returning the Light

and

Guarding-Keeping the

Center

Where did the term "Returning the Light" come from?

It began with the True Man Wenshi*.

* Wenshi (文始), also known as Yin Xi (尹喜). According to the legends, he was the guard who recognized Lao Zi when he wanted to cross the border and became one of the first disciples. He is also the author of the text Guan Yinzi (關尹子), also known as Wenshi Zhēnjīng (文始真經) and it has nine chapters. In chapter five, there is a saying, "譬如两目，能见天地万物，暂时回光," which means "For instance, with two eyes, you can see Heaven, Earth, and all things, and at the right time you can Return the Light."

When the Light is Returned, then the Qi-Energy of Heaven and Earth, Yin and Yang are all congealed.

This is what is also called "Refined thought," "Pure Qi-Energy," or "Pure thought."

When you start following this art, then (you will find that) in Being there is Non-Being.

After a long time of practice, you will succeed and have the (true) body beyond your (physical) body;

it is Being within Non-being.**

** In the meaning of "create something from nothing."

After a hundred days* of special work, the Light becomes True, and it will be the Fire of Spirit-Shen.

* "A hundred days" is the traditional term for building the foundation. Actually, it does not necessarily take the actual hundred days and you usually need more time to complete this stage.

After a hundred days, the Light will naturally condense within, and one point of True Yang will produce a small pearl.

It is similar to how a man and a woman conceive a child after sexual intercourse.

After that, you have to remain in calmness and wait, Returning the Light.

This is what is also called "Fire Times-periods."*

* Fire Times-periods are very important in Daoist Cultivation. In other words, you should do every step at the right time. It is like cooking food

when each ingredient should be added at the right time; otherwise, it will be impossible to eat. This is why the terminology of internal alchemy is basically derived from external alchemy, where herbs, mushrooms, minerals, and other substances were used to create medicine. In external alchemy, if you add the correct ingredient at the wrong time, it will be useless or even become a poison, depending on the level of your medicine.

Among the original transformations, there is Yang Light, which is the main ruler.

In the physical world, it is the Sun; in the human body, it is the eyes.

It leads to the scattering/dissemination Spirit-Shen and its qualities, which is the worst.

That is why the Dao-Way of the Golden Flower uses the reverse method**.

** There are two ways: From the One to Many and From Many to the One. "From the One to Many" is clockwise direction; it is also called "from the root to the branches" or "forward way." "From Many to the One" is the counterclockwise direction; it is also called "from the branches to the root" or "reverse way." This principle was also mentioned in Dao De Jing by Lao Zi: "Those who go backward are going to Dao"; therefore, "Those who learn - gain every day, Those who follow the Dao-Way - lose every day."

Returning the Light - you should know that this is not only returning the essence/quintessence of the single whole body but also returning the True Qi-Energy of the entire creation.

It is not only for stopping ignorance and delusions but also to get rid of reincarnation.

Therefore, each breath corresponds to one year of human time and a hundred years in the "nine-level endless night in hell."

After ordinary people are born screaming, they pursue objects of sense perception and live under their influence.

They never look at it as a bad thing, and eventually, their Yang Qi-Energy becomes weaker until they die and enter the realm of the nine dark hells.

That is why Léngyán Jīng says: "If you can keep the pure idea-intention, you will be able to ascend; if you keep/follow the pure desire/emotion, you will fall/degrade."

If disciples have few thoughts but many desires, they will be submerged into inferior Ways.

Only through internal observation in a state of deep calmness can you achieve success and become enlightened*.

This is the reverse method that is used here.

* 正觉 (zhèngjué) is a Chinese term for the Sanskrit word "samadhi." 正 means "right, proper, correct," and 觉 means "awake, wake up, become aware/awakened." Therefore, I translated it as enlightened.

Yīnfú Jing** says: "The mechanism is in the eyes."

** Yīnfú Jing (阴符经), also known as Huangdi Yinfu Ling or "Scripture on Hidden Talismans by Emperor Huang Di." There are two versions of Huangdi Yinfujing, a shorter text containing about 300+ characters and a longer text containing approximately 400+ characters, in three sections. A longer version was translated in Book 9.

"Huang Di Su Wen* says: "The essence/quintessence of the human body flows upwards into the orifice of the emptiness."

* Huang Di Su Wen (黄帝素问), also known as Huáng Dì Nèi Jīng Sù Wèn (黄帝内经素问) or "Inner Canon of the Yellow Emperor," and Suwen (素问) means "Simple Questions."

If you can realize it, you can achieve longevity, and ascension (to Heaven) also depends on it. This is the art of implementation of the Three Teachings.**

** Three Teachings - Confucianism, Buddhism, and Daoism.

The Light is neither inside nor outside of the body.

Mountains, rivers, the Sun, the Moon, and the whole Earth shine and illuminate, this is all Light.

Therefore, the Light is not only inside the body.

The brightness of your mind, keen intelligence, cleverness, and wisdom are all active, and all of this is Light.

Therefore, the Light is not only outside the body.

The Light of Heaven and Earth fills the boundless universe.

The Light of one body can also naturally fill Heaven and cover the Earth.

Therefore, as soon as you Return the Light - Heaven, Earth, mountains, rivers, and everything in the world will also be returned.

The essence/quintessence of a person flows upwards into the eyes; this is the great key to the (Mysterious) Gate in the human body.

You should think about it*, because if you do not practice meditation** for one day, who knows where the Light is flowing and where it will stop?

* This saying can also be translated as "Children, take attention to it."

** The term used was Jìng zuò (静坐) which literally means "sit quietly" and is also one of the terms for meditation.

If you can meditate for a short time, you will be able to understand it even if you have already lived thousands of kalpas*.

* A kalpa is an extremely long period of time, generally between the creation and re-creation of the universe.

All methods return to quietness; it is truly unimaginable, incomprehensible, and mysterious.

Nevertheless, you have to start your practice from simple/obvious to profound, from rough/crude to subtle.

The most important thing is to be consistent, then it will be marvelous.

Mastery is when you are consistent from beginning to end.

But in the process of practice, you know whether you are warm or cold, and you can only experience it personally.

In short, you have to reach the state "as wide as the sea and as vast as the sky" and "all things remain in Suchness*."

Only this can be considered a success in (Cultivation).

* Suchness is the essential nature of phenomenal existence, the nature of reality free from conceptual elaborations and the subject-object distinction.

Since ancient times, the masters and sages have transmitted their knowledge and never stepped out of the reverse observation.

Confucians call it "attain/acquire knowledge," Buddhists call it "observing heart-mind," and Daoists call it "inner observation."

It is all the same.

However, people know these two words, "reverse observation," but they still cannot succeed because they do not understand the true meaning of these two words.

"Reverse" means comprehension of your own heart-mind.

"Reverse" is when you return to the stage when the body and Spirit-Shen have not yet manifested.

Therefore, in my six-foot-tall body, I should return my attention and ask, "What was my true form before Heaven and Earth were born?"

However, modern people can meditate for one or two hours*, they return their attention and think only of themselves and their personal behavior and call it "reverse observation."

How can they even hope to succeed!?

* Look at the duration of meditation. It does not say 20-30 minutes, it says "one or two hours". The duration of meditation is also crucial because some transformations cannot be done for less time. That is why you should keep quality meditation for a long time.

The founders of Buddhism and Daoism taught people "to look at the tip of their noses."

This does not mean that you should focus on the tip of the nose or look at the tip of the nose.

You should keep your thought among/within the "Yellow."**

** It indicates the "Yellow Woman," which is True Intention. Therefore, it means that you have to form the True Intention for correct Cultivation.

Wherever your eyes go, the heart-mind also follows there.

How can you look up and down at the same time?

How can your (mind) be unstable/uncertain about up and down?

It is like confusing the finger pointed at the moon with the moon itself.

How is this even possible?

When they say the words "tip of the nose," it indicates the Marvelous-Mysterious.

You should rely on your nose and use your eyes as a standard/rule*.

* Nose is in the middle of the face, starting from the place between the eyes. Therefore, you should use it as a finger pointing to the moon, where the nose and eyes are "the finger," and the upper dantian is "the moon."

The original (true intention) is not on the nose.

If your eyes are too wide open, then you can see too far and not be able to see the nose.

If your eyes are locked/closed too tightly, then your eyes are closed and you won't be able to see your nose.

When the eyes are opened too wide, your attention is easily distracted/scattered outward.

When the eyes are locked/closed too tightly, your attention will chase dreams and easily become chaotic and confused.

Only if your eyes are moderately and appropriately closed can you see the tip of the nose so that you can use it as a standard.

In this way, you can let the Light come in naturally, and you don't have to use force/take the initiative to bring it in or out.

Looking at the tip of the nose is only the very beginning of entering a state of Calmness.

Open your eyes and take a look, realize the standard/ set the criterion/guiding line, and then let it be.

It is like a bricklayer using thread (as a plumb line).

When a bricklayer sets to work, he hangs up the thread and guides himself by it, without bothering to look at the plumb line constantly.

Zhǐ Guān* is a Buddhist method that has never been a secret.

* Zhǐ Guān (止观) means "Cessation/Stopping and Observation/ Contemplation" and is used as the primary method in the Chinese Buddhist school Tiantai (天台). Zhǐ Guān is the Chinese word for the Sanskrit term "Śamatha-vipaśyanā."

Use both your eyes to look at the tip of the nose while sitting in the correct-upright position in a state of calm and holding the heart-mind focused in accordance with the Middle**.

** "The Middle," in other words, the Middle Way, which avoids the extremes of sensual indulgence and self-abasement.

This does not necessarily mean the "middle of the head"; however, it will be good if you impartially focus your thought-intention on the place between the eyes.

The Light will become active, and you only need to focus the thought-intention on the spot between the eyes, then the Light will penetrate naturally.

It is not necessary to keep the attention on the Central Castle.

These few words of mine covered the main idea (of this method).

As for other details of entry and exit in the state of Calmness, what you should do before and after, you can refer to the book "Xiǎo Zhi Guan"* for confirmation and verification.

* "Xiǎo Zhi Guan," or "Small Treatise on Cessation/Stopping and Observation/Contemplation," was written by Zhiyi (智顗), the fourth patriarch of the Tiantai school, who lived in 538-597.

The words "Focus in accordance with the Middle" are the most miraculous.

"The Middle" - the whole boundless universe can be included in it and indicates the mechanism of the entire creation.

Thus, you must enter this gate.

"Focus in accordance with" is the key, the starting point, but that does not mean that you should be attached to it.

The meaning of these words ("Focus in accordance with the Middle") is so profound and marvelous.

The words "Zhǐ Guān" cannot be separated, it is a contemplation and wisdom.

In the future, if any thoughts arise, do not sit rigidly but investigate your thoughts.

Where do they come from?

How do they arise?

Where do they go?

Repeat this investigation again and again until you realize that it cannot be grasped, then you (have a chance) to see where thoughts arise.

After that, you should no longer try to find the source of the thought, because you have already reached the state of "Looking for the heart-mind and realizing that it cannot be grasped" and "I will calm your heart-mind for you."*

* These last two statements are taken from the stories about the second patriarch of Chan Buddhism, Huike (慧可), who lived in 487-593. It is called "Huike and Pacifying the Mind." The story is as follows: Huike said to Bodhidharma, "My mind is not peaceful. Could you pacify it?" Bodhidharma replied, "Bring me your mind, and I will pacify it." Huike said, "I tried to find it, but I realized that it cannot be grasped." Bodhidharma replied, "I have already calmed your mind for you."

This is the right observation.

What is contrary to this is false observation.

When you reach the state of "it cannot be grasped"**, then (if there will be new thoughts) continuously Cease them, and then Observe them, Observation and Cessation.

** The state of "it cannot be grasped" means that you cannot find your mind.

This is the Dual Cultivation of contemplation and wisdom.

This is the Returning the Light.

The Returning is Cessation/Stopping, and the Light is Observation.

Cessation/Stopping without Observation is called Returning without the Light; Observation without Cessation/Stopping is called having the Light without Returning.

Keep it in mind.

Chapter 4

Returning the Light

And

Breathing Regulation

The main idea is to maintain the heart-mind pure and purposeful during practice.

You don't have to strive for results and results will come naturally*.

* This is a fundamental rule and key to success in Cultivation. If you want something too much, then you are less likely to get it. It happens because your strong desire will be the obstacle on your way to that thing. As soon as you put that desire away, there will be no obstacle anymore and you will get it naturally. This is also called "Desire without desire." But if you have no desire at all, you will never achieve it, which is another side of this mistake. Neither "desire" nor "not desire," this is the key.

In general, beginners have two vices: drowsiness and distraction.

The way to get rid of them, you should not become attached to the heart-mind and the breath.

The word "breath" consists of two characters "self/from" and "heart-mind."**

** The character 息 (xī) means breath, where the upper part is 自 (zì) means "self/from," and the lower part is 心 (xīn) means "heart-mind."

Thus, "from the heart-mind" is the breath.

When the heart-mind moves, Qi-Energy appears; therefore, Qi-Energy comes from the heart-mind.

Our thoughts appear very quickly, delusions occur in a flash, and the breath responds to them.*

* It means that our heart-mind generates thoughts that give rise to feelings and emotions and affect breathing. Remember how you breathe when you are angry or sad. This is the best proof of the above words.

Therefore, there is inner and outer breathing; it is like sound and echo following each other.

In one day, we have thousands of inhales and exhales, so they give rise to thousands of delusional thoughts.

The brightness of the Spirit-Shen will be completely depleted and become like wither wood and cold ashes.

So should a person not have thoughts?

But a person cannot be without thoughts.

It is like saying you should not breathe, but you cannot be without breathing.

It is better to turn this disease into medicine when the breath and the heart-mind rely on each other and are interdependent.

Therefore, Returning the Light should include breathing regulation.

This method uses Light.

It is the Light of the eyes and the Light of the ears.

The Light of the eyes is the Light of the outer sun and moon; the Light of the ears is the Light of the united Essence-Jing of the internal sun and moon.

However, Essence-Jing is the condensed Light, "They both come from the same source but have different names*."

* This is a quote from the first chapter of Dao De Jing by Lao Zi.

Therefore, sensitive (hearing) and clear (sight) unite into one Spiritual Light.

During meditation, lower your eyelids, set a standard, and then let go.

But if you completely let go of the situation, you cannot keep your heart-mind on listening to your breath at the same time.

When you inhale and exhale, you should not hear your breath, only listen to its soundlessness.

Even if there is a tiny sound, it means that your breathing is rough and not yet subtle enough / cannot penetrate into subtle.

You need to be patient and act gradually.

The more you free it, the more subtle it becomes; the more subtle it becomes, the deeper the calm.

Eventually, even subtle breathing will suddenly stop, and then True Breathing will appear.

At that moment, you can comprehend the essence/ original face of yourself.

Therefore, the more subtle your heart-mind, the more subtle your breath.

When the heart-mind is unified, then Qi-Energy moves.

When breathing is subtle, then the heart-mind is also subtle.

When Qi-Energy is unified, then it mobilizes the heart-mind.

If you want to stabilize your heart-mind, you need first to Cultivate your Qi-Energy; otherwise, the heart-mind has nothing to start working with.

Therefore, Qi Cultivation is the starting point; it is also called "Keeping Pure Qi-Energy."

Your generation still does not understand the meaning of the word "movement."

"Movement" is a keyword, it is also another name for "Control".

Using vigorous activity can cause movement, then why (the heart-mind) cannot be calmed by pure stillness!?

The great sages knew that Qi-Energy and the heart-mind depend on each other and skillfully used it for the benefit of future generations.

Alchemy books say, "The hen is embracing the egg, and using the heart-mind, always listening to it."

This is the essential key.

A hen can give life to an egg through the Qi-Energy of warmth.

Qi-Energy of warmth only can heat the shell but cannot penetrate inside.

That is why the hen uses the heart-mind to direct the Qi-Energy inward.

The listening is purposefully/single-minded concentration.

If the heart-mind can penetrate, so can Qi-Energy, and Qi-Energy of warmth can give life.

Therefore, although the hen leaves from time to time, the Spirit-Shen is focused and always keeps the Qi-Energy of warmth on the eggs day and night.

Because it is never interrupted, therefore the Spirit-Shen (inside the egg) awakes to life.

The Spirit-Shen becomes alive due to the prior death of the heart-mind.

If a person can refuse the heart-mind, the Original Spirit-Shen awakes to life.

To refuse the heart-mind does not mean being withered and stupid, but purposeful and not divided.

Buddha said: "Put your heart-mind in the same place, and there will be nothing that cannot be done."*

* This is a quote from Yíjiào Jing (遗教经). This is the last instruction given by Buddha to his disciples before Nirvana, explaining the precepts, concentration, and wisdom that are the foundation of Buddhism. It has twenty-one chapters.

The heart-mind is easy to lose, so you need to merge it with Qi-Energy.

Qi-Energy is easy to become rough, then use the heart-mind to make it subtle and refined.

Therefore, how can you be unstable and unbalanced?

Generally, there are two vices: drowsiness and distraction.

You need to practice the Art of Calmness every day continuously, and you will naturally achieve the cessation of breathing and quietness.

If you are not practicing meditation (Jìng zuò), there will still be distractions, you just will not notice them.

When you are aware of your distractions, it becomes a mechanism to eliminate them.

Drowsiness that you are not aware of and drowsiness that you are aware of are not the same thing; in fact, they are a thousand miles apart.

The drowsiness that is not noticed is true drowsiness.

If you notice your drowsiness, it is not total drowsiness because there is still clarity in it.

Distraction is when your Spirit-Shen is somewhere else; drowsiness is when your Spirit-Shen is unclear.

Distraction is easy to heal, but drowsiness is difficult.

It's like being sick.

If there is pain or itching, it can be cured by taking the right medicine; but drowsiness is like an unconscious paralysis.

If you are scattered, you can be collected; if you are confused, you can be put in order; but if you have drowsiness, you are in formless ignorance.

At least the distraction has some direction, but drowsiness is when the Po-Souls take full advantage of you.

Distraction is when there are just Po-Souls, but drowsiness is when pure Yin (of Po-Souls) is your ruler.

If you feel sleepy during meditation, it is drowsiness, but it can be cured by regulating breathing.

Although the breath here is just an ordinary inhale and exhale, and it is not True Breath, it nevertheless contains the inhale and exhale of True Breath.

During meditation, you need to calm your heart-mind and purify the Qi-Energy.

How to calm the heart-mind?

You have to use your breath, just breathe in and out, and have the intention of the heart-mind to comprehend yourself.

You should not be able to hear your breathing, if you do not hear it, then it is subtle; if it is subtle, then it is clear/clean.

If you are able to hear your breathing, then your Qi-Energy is rough; if it is rough, then it is turbid.

If it is turbid, then you will have drowsiness and fall asleep.

This is a natural way.

If you keep your heart-mind on the breath, then you can master it.

This is the principle of "Using without using" - just keep light and subtle (reverse) observation-lighting and listening.

What does "observation-lighting" mean?

It is the Light of the eyes that naturally illuminate.

Eyes only look inward and not outward, and since the eyes do not look outward but yet vigilant, it is called "inner observation."

But still, that does not mean you are really/actually looking inward.

What does "listening" mean?

It is the Light of the ears that naturally listens.

Ears only listen inward and not outward, and since the ears do not listen outward but yet vigilant, it is called "inner listening."

But still, that does not mean you are really/actually listening inward.

Listening is when you listen to the soundless; observation is when you observe the formless.

When the eyes do not look outward and the ears do not listen outward, then they are locked up and tend to run around inside.

Only with "inner observation" and "inner listening," neither traveling outside (in the state of mind) nor running around inside, in the state of "in-between," can you prevent drowsiness.

This is how the sun and the moon merge their Essence-Jing and the Light.

When you feel drowsiness, just get up and take a walk.

After your Spirit-Shen clears up, sit down again.

When you wake up early in the morning, you will have free time, so this is the best time to meditate with an incense stick.

In the afternoon, people have things to do and a lot of distractions, so it is easy to fall into drowsiness.

There is no need to limit the time of meditation with an incense stick; all you need is to put aside all distractions and practice meditation for a while.

Eventually, you will make progress, achieve immersion and never feel drowsiness again.

Chapter 5

Mistakes in

Returning the Light

Although your mastery becomes better and more advanced, still "there are many pitfalls in front of the cliff of withered trees."

I will explain it to you in detail.

When you can reach these levels, you will be able to understand this information, which is why I am explaining it now.

My school and Chan school* are not the same, my school has step-by-step verification of effectiveness.

* Denotes the school of Chan Buddhism, better known in the West as Zen Buddhism, which is a Japanese variation of pronunciation.

Let me tell you about the differences first, and then we will talk about the verification of effectiveness.

When you are going to practice at my school, you should first prepare yourself.

This means that you should not put too much effort into it, and be fresh/vigilant and free.

Your Qi-Energy should be in harmony and the heart-mind should be calm.

Then you can immerse into a deep Stillness/Meditation.

To make Stillness correct, you should find the right mechanism and the proper way to enter it/its opening.

You should not sit in a state of "doing nothing,"* which is also called "not remembering anything."

* This state is also known as "Stupid sitting." It is when you sit without any intention, just sit and wait for something, but without True Intention, it will lead to nothing but stupidity.

When you let everything go, you still should be clearheaded and composed.

You should not be too enthusiastic or take everything too seriously.

It is easy to fall into these traps.

Neither "perceiving reality" nor "not perceiving reality;" between existence and non-existence; in a

state of "in-between," you can get the state of "having intention without intention.*"

* Which also means True Intention.

If you have fresh/vigilant awareness, then you can naturally let go.

But do not let go totally, otherwise you will fall into the Realm of Aggregates where five evils rule.**

** 蘊 (yùn) is usually translated as "accumulate, hold in store, contain," but it is also a Chinese term for the Sanskrit word "Skandha," which means "heaps, aggregates, collections, groupings." In other words, it is aggregates of clinging. There are Five Skandhas or Five aggregates of clinging: form (or material image), sensations (or feelings received from the form), perceptions, mental activity or formations, and consciousness.

If you have a tendency to immerse into a state of "wither trees and cold ashes," it means you have a lack of Yang power.

It also means that you are entering the realm of Yin power.

It has a cold Qi/passive mood, breathing becomes heavy, and there are many other signs of coldness and decay.

Eventually, you will become an insensitive blockhead.

Also, you cannot simply follow all mental things and states*.

* 缘 (yuán) is usually translated as "hem, margin, reason, cause, fate," but it is also a Chinese term for the Sanskrit word "Pratyaya," which refers to the causes of mental activity. Therefore, it is an auxiliary, indirect cause, as distinguished from a direct cause. Take, for example, the seed, which is the direct cause of the plant, while sunlight, water, and earth are the indirect causes of the plant. Sometimes Pratyaya means the cause in general.

During meditation, you may find that different thoughts come one after another without any reason, and you are not able to get rid of them; but by following them, you may find it easier and more comfortable.

It's called the "Master becoming a slave."

Eventually, you will get bogged down in the worlds of the Realm of Desire.

If you are lucky, you will be born in Heaven (of the Realm of Desire); if you are unlucky, you will be born as a cat; if you are neither "lucky" nor "unlucky," you will be born as a Fairy Fox*.

* Fairy fox is Chinese mythological creatures that are usually shape-shifting that can be an either a good or evil spirit. In Chinese mythology, the Fairy Fox can take many forms with different meanings, powers, and characteristics.

As the Fairy Fox, you will enjoy the wind and moon, flowers and fruits, and grow the Precious-miraculous plant** in the famous mountains.

** 瑶草 (yáocǎo) is a plant with miraculous powers that can cure all diseases and give longevity.

You will enjoy your lifestyle for three to five hundred years and sometimes even thousands of years.

But in the end, you will still be reborn in another world of Samsara.

All of these are the wrong paths.

If you know the wrong ways, then you can seek verification of effectiveness.

Chapter 6

Returning the Light
and
Verification of
Effectiveness

There are many verifications of effectiveness, but they cannot be passed by people with small roots/ superficial people and with small vessels/narrow-minded people.

You must think about the liberation of all beings, and you cannot do it with carelessness and arrogance but only in accordance with what I said above.

The state of Stillness and Calmness should be continuous and without interruption, the Spirit-Shen and mood should be upraised, as if you were drunk or taking a bath.

It is called "Yang (power) in harmony throughout the whole body and the Golden Flower suddenly blooms."

Afterward, the next state, "no sound to be heard and a full moon in the sky," appears, and you feel that the whole earth is completely filled with light and has become the Realm of Light.

This is the symbol of the enlightening of the heart-mind and body, the correct release of the Golden Flower.

After a while, the whole body will be filled, and you will not be afraid of wind and frost.

When other people encounter something uninterested, my Spirit-Shen shines even brighter.

It is like a house built of gold, like a terrace built of white jade.

In a world where things get rotten, I use the True Qi-Energy to bring them back to life.

The red blood turns into milk and the body of flesh into golden treasure.

This is the Great Condensation/Stabilization of the Golden Flower.

The first stage corresponds to the images of "Guān Wú Liàng Shòu Jīng,"* such as "sunset," "big body of water," and "row of trees."

* Guān Wú Liàng Shòu Jīng (观无量寿经) is also known as 佛說觀無量壽佛經 or Amitayurdhyana Sutra, which can be translated as "Sutra on the Observation of the Buddha of Immeasurable Life." It is a Mahayana sutra in Pure Land Buddhism, a branch of Chinese Mahayana Buddhism.

"Sunset" symbolizes that in the Chaos the foundation is being built by the Wuji-Limitless.

"Supreme kindness is like water"* is the flawless purity of Taiji/Great Limit, the established ruler, which is also called "The Emperor comes from the East."**

* This phrase is the first line of the eighth chapter of the Dao De Jing.

** The meaning of this phrase is explained in the commentary on the Yi Jing (易经) or the Book of Changes. It means that the Celestial Emperor created all things and began to use Qi from the East, which symbolizes Spring, and it is also the place of the Thunder trigram in the Post Celestial Ba Gua circle.

Thunder trigram also belongs to the Wood Phase***, and it is represented by a "row of trees."

Trees standing in seven rows symbolize the Light of the seven orifices****.

*** Wood Phase is one of the Five Phases (Wu Xing). You can find more information and their correlations in Book 1.

**** Seven orifices are the eyes, ears, nostrils, and mouth, which are also related to their abilities, such as sight, hearing, smell, and taste.

In the Northwest is the Qián trigram, then Kan trigram.

Sunset over the body of water is the image of the Qián trigram and Kan trigram.

Kan trigram is Zǐ time (midnight) and Winter Solstice.

On the day of the Winter Solstice, the thunder hides in the Earth and little by little rumbles more and more, and when Yang (power) comes out, the Thunder trigram appears, which symbolizes a "row of trees."

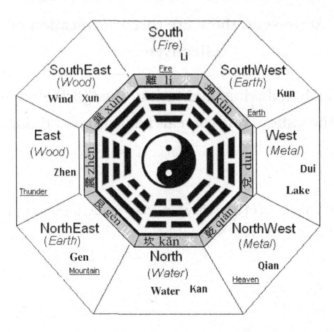

The rest can be deduced by analogy.

The second stage is based on the state that can be described as "Everything around is frozen and turned into a colorful treasure place where the brightness of Light gradually condensed."

Then you can see the image of the terrace and Buddha.

It means that the Golden Original Nature manifests, and Buddha is the Great Awakening of the Golden Immortal.

It describes the verification of effectiveness in general terms.

At present, there are three verification of effectiveness.

One is when during meditation, the Spirit-Shen enters the valley* but you can hear others talking.

* Indicates on "spirit of the valley," in other words, the area of the Upper Dantian.

As if a mile away, but everything is clear, although all reaching sounds are like an echo in the valley.

Everything is heard (but as if) you yourself have never heard anything.

This is called the Spirit-Shen in the valley, and you can experience it at any time and get proof for yourself.

One is when you are in a state of Stillness and Calmness, the Light of the eyes rises, fills, and appears before you in the form of white Light.

It is like when you open your eyes among the clouds and try to find your body, but you cannot find it.

This is called "Light appears in the empty room."

Everything inside and outside is well-illuminated; this is a favorable sign.

One is when you are in a state of Stillness and Calmness, the base of the carnal body becomes very subtle, like silk or jade.

It is like during sitting meditation you feel that you are unable to keep sitting because of the feeling that you are rising and floating.

This is called "Spirit-Shen returns to Heaven."

Eventually, you can achieve ascension.

Now you can use these three as verifications for your results.

It's fair to say that it is impossible to describe fully in words because everyone has different natural inclinations and abilities, and depending on them, people can experience various manifestations.

As is said in "Zhi Guan Book*": "Good roots manifest the same appearance."

* Zhi Guan method was already mentioned in Chapter 3.

It is like only the person who drinks water knows whether it is cold or warm.

It has to be your own experience, and then it will be true.

Pre-Celestial Qi-Energy becomes one/unified and is in the present moment, and it can be used as a personal verification of effectiveness.

74

When Qi united, you can create the Elixir.

This one small grain of Elixir is the True pearl.

One grain after another, from fuzziness to notable.**

** This line is from the Zhang Boduan (张伯端) text "Four Hundred Words of the Golden Elixir" (金丹四百字).

The Pre-Celestial (Qi-Energy) gradually condenses and eventually turns into one grain (of Elixir), where all qualities of the Pre-Celestial (state) are presented.

This grain is measureless, boundless, and without any limitations.

Each grain has the power of a grain (of the Elixir).

This is the essential principle, and you have to be determined.

Chapter 7

The Living Method
of
Returning the Light

Following the method of Returning the Light, you do not need to give up on your usual activity.

The ancients said: "When things/affairs come, you have to respond appropriately to them; when things come, you have to see through them*."

* "To see through them" means seeing their true sense.

In everyday affairs, you must keep the right intention, then the Light will not follow things, but the Light will return.

This is called the "Endless repetition of the formless Returning the Light."

If you can do that, then you will have the True, correct, and noticeable** Returning the Light.

** Noticeable means that other people will feel your deepness and that you are an unusual person.

You should be able to practice the reverse shining* in everyday affairs without seeing the difference between others and yourself.

* Reverse shining is just another term for Returning the Light.

If you can practice Returning the Light anytime and anywhere, it will be a marvelous use of the main idea/ principle.

In the early morning, you should eliminate all kinds of distractions and sit quietly/meditate for an hour or two - that is the best.

Every time you are involved in everyday affairs, you should use the reverse shining method, then there will be no interruption.

If you can practice this for two-three months, then the True celestial beings will come to you to validate your results.

Chapter 8

The Secret Method

of

Carefree Wandering

Jade Purity left the Secret Method of Carefree Wandering, only a few words "Condensed Spirit-Shen enters the Qi Orifice*."

In the summer, you suddenly see flying white snow, and at midnight the red sun**.

A gentle wind rises among the water, you are floating in heaven and returning to feeding on the Virtue of Earth***.

There is one more line - "mysterious within a mysterious," - the Land of Nothingness is the True Abode****.

* Heaven of Jade Purity (玉清 - Yù Qīng) is the sphere where Yuanshi Tianzun (元始天尊) resides. Jade Purity is one of the "Three Purities," and Yuanshi Tianzun is one of the "Three Pure Ones." Three Pure Ones are the three highest deities of the Daoist religion. The other two are Lingbao Tianzun (靈寶天尊) and Daode Tianzun (道德天尊). Lingbao Tianzun governs the Heaven of Shang Qing (上清) or High Purity. Daode Tianzun governs the Heaven of Tai Qing (太清) or Great Purity.

Qi Orifice has several meanings. It could be the upper Dantian or the Mysterious Gate, and it will depend on the context.

** "Flying white snow" is also called "Light appears in the empty room," and it was explained in Chapter 6. "At midnight" signifies a deep state of Stillness and Calmness. "The red sun" means that True Yang Qi is born.

*** "A gentle wind rises among the water" means soft and gentle abdominal breathing can raise your Spirit-Shen, and you will experience the state of "floating in heaven." "The Virtue of Earth" indicates being humble, modest, grounded, sensible, and other similar qualities.

**** "Mysterious within a mysterious" comes from Chapter 1 of Dao De Jing: "The Mystery within a Mystery/the Mystery of Mysteries is the gateway of all the Mysterious-Wonderful." This state is a key to Mysterious Gate.

"The Land of Nothingness" is an idiom from Zhuāng Zǐ (庄子): "今子有大树，患其无用，何不树之于无何有之乡，广莫之野, 彷徨乎无为其侧，逍遥乎寝卧其下.," meaning: "Now you have a big tree and worry about its useless, why not plant it in the land of nothingness, in the wilderness of vastness, carefree wandering around the tree doing nothing, or sleep under it?"

This poem thoroughly explains the Mysterious and Profound.

The essence of the Great Dao-Way does not go beyond the scope of the words "Doing through Non-Doing."

Only Non-Doing is the reason why a person does not attach to limited categories/conventions, forms, and images.

Only Non-Doing is the reason why a person does not immerse in the "stupid emptiness and dead void."

The function does not go beyond the word "Center," and the main mechanism is in the eyes.

The eyes are like the handle of the Big Dipper that determines/governs creation and transformations and manages Yin and Yang.

From beginning to end, the Great Medicine is only the "metal within water" where water is the dwelling for the lead*.

* More information about Lead and Mercury, Water and Fire, Dragon and Tiger, etc., you can find in "Chapters on Awakening to the True Reality" (悟真篇) by Daoist Master Zhang Boduan (张伯端). It was translated in Book 6.

The foregoing discussion of the Returning the Light is used to guide beginners to control the inside from the

outside; it's like a vassal coming to be approved by the emperor.

This is for middle and low-level people who cultivate the two lower passes to penetrate the upper pass*.

* The basic rule: you must consider yourself a middle or low-level student. It means that you have to start with the methods of Building the Foundation, then move on to the first stage and the second stage, which are called "Cultivating Essence-Jing into Qi-Energy" and "Cultivating Qi-Energy into Spirit-Shen." I understand that not a lot of people want to be low-level or middle-level students, but you cannot enter a university without school knowledge. I am also aware that some students consider themselves high-level students, but 99% of them are not. In most cases, it simply means that the student is having a problem with recognizing his actual level. It is like a kid who decided to go to university but has not even finished high school yet. He can try, but he will not pass the tests, and he will have to go back to school, and he will lose time. This is a very common mistake and not many students can recognize it.

The upper stage also has two levels: "Cultivating the Spirit to return to the Emptiness" and "Cultivating the Emptiness to merge with the Dao."

Now the main sequence of the path has been clarified, and the mechanism is gradually becoming ready.

Heaven does not care about the Dao-Way, (that is why I) directly reveal the highest ideas/principles of Teaching.

All of you should keep them a secret and make every effort (for their realization).

Returning the Light is a general name.

With every new level of this art, the Light also increases and becomes more subtle.

Earlier, we talked about how you can control the inside from the outside; now, you are within and should control the outside.

Before, it was like a vassal coming to be approved by the emperor; now, it is like the emperor gives orders with respect - everything is in reverse.

If you want to immerse in Stillness and Calmness, first regulate and maintain your body and the heart-mind.

You should be free from any doubts, be in peace and harmony, and let go of principal and secondary causes so that nothing can stick to you.

When the Heart-Mind of Heaven takes the right place in the center, then lower your eyes as if receiving the imperial edict for summoning the ministers.

Who dares to disobey?

After, use your eyes for the inner illumination of the Palace of Kan-Water*, the shining of the Light appears, and True Yang comes out in response.

* Palace of Kan-Water is an area of the lower Dantian.

Li-Fire trigram has Yang (lines) outside and Yin (line) inside - it is a body/substance for the Qian-Heaven trigram.

That one Yin (line) inside, which rules the (Li-Fire trigram), causes the heart-mind to follow things and return to the routine of Samsara.

But when you practice Returning the Light for inner illumination, the heart-mind does not follow things, and Yin is under control.

When the shining of the Light pours and illuminates, the pure Yang occurs.

坤
Kun (Earth) Gen (Mountain) Kan (Water) Xun (Wind)

震
Zhen (Thunder) Li (Fire) Dui (Lake) Qian (Heaven)

According to the principle "Like attracts like," the Yang (line) in the Kan-Water trigram rises up.

Therefore, this Yang (line) does not belong to the Kan-Water trigram but to the Qian-Heaven trigram and corresponds to Yang in it.

When these two things meet, then they are tied and inseparable, in interaction and living movement, coming and going, floating and sinking.

At this time, inside the Original Palace, there is the boundless and immeasurable Great Emptiness, and the whole body seems light, marvelous, and soaring.

This is called "Clouds filling a thousand mountains."

After that, the (mechanism of) coming and going is without a trace, the (principle of) floating and sinking is indistinguishable.

Suddenly the meridians become steady/solid and the Qi-Energy suspends; this is True copulate.

It is also called "Moon reflected in thousands of waters."

When in the midst of the (mysterious) darkness, suddenly the Heart-Mind of Heaven moves slightly; it is a sign that Yang has returned at the live Zi time (midnight).

But this information should be explained in detail.

Ordinary people see with their eyes and listen with their ears.

Their eyes and ears chase things and therefore become active.

When the things are gone, the seeing and listening are over.

This activity and rest are characteristic of ordinary people, and it is like the rightful emperor becomes a slave.

This is also tantamount to living with ghosts.

But if during any activity and rest, you still remain in Heaven* while you are among people, then the Emperor of Heaven is a True Man.

* It means that your True Intention is aimed at comprehending the Innermost Sence and the Mysterious Spirituality of the Original Reality.

When there is movement, everything moves with it; it is called the "Root of Heaven."

When there is a rest, everything is resting with it; this type of rest is called a "Moon Cave."

Its movement and the rest have no cause and everything moves and rest without a cause.

When it rests from top to bottom, everything also rests from top to bottom.

This is also called "The Root of Heaven and the Moon Cave freely come and go."

When the Heart-Mind of Heaven is in a state of Stillness and Calmness and (the mechanism of Qi)

moves too early, then you will lose tenderness/softness (of the Fire times-periods).

When the Heart-Mind of Heaven is already moving, and (the mechanism of Qi) is moving later, then it will be too late/stale (for the Fire times-periods).

(The right way is) when the Heart-Mind of Heaven just starts to move slightly, you should use True Intention to raise (your Qi-Energy) to the Palace of Qian-Heaven and use the Spiritual Light (of your eyes) to observe the top of your head.

This is the proper guidance and action at the correct time.

When the Heart-Mind of Heaven reaches the top of the Palace of Qian-Heaven, you will experience floating/soaring until suddenly it stops due to immersing into a deep Calmness.

Then, you should quickly use the True Intention to move (Qi-Energy) down to the Huáng Tíng/Yellow Court,* and observe the spiritual place within with the Light of your eyes.

---

* Huáng Tíng or Yellow Court is the name of the middle Dantian.

After that, you will immerse into a deep Calmness again, and not a single thought will be born.

While inner observation, you suddenly forget about observation, then the body and the heart-mind achieve the Great Liberation, and all kinds of feelings and thousands of thoughts disappear.

Then you will not be able to recognize the spiritual place, furnace and caldron; even if you try to find your body, you will not be able to do it.

This state is called "Heaven enters the Earth," and that is the moment when all wonders* return to the root.

* Wonders mean different phenomena that you can only imagine and experience.

It is also called "Condensed Spirit-Shen enters the Qi Orifice."

When you only start practicing Returning the Light, (your heart-mind) is scattered, but it needs to be collected, and the six senses should be stopped.

This is called "Cultivate the Original Source and add fuel to Vitality-Ming."

After (the Light) is converged/collected, you will naturally experience carefree soaring and you don't have to put in any effort for it.

This state is called "Calmed Spirit-Shen in Ancestor Orifice and Gathering Pre-Celestial."

Then, all influences gradually disappear, and you enter a state of "Profound Quietness of the Great Calmness."

It is also called "Hibernate in the Qi hole/cave and return all wonders to the source/root."

One method has three stages and each stage has nine sections.

I will explain it to you in detail later.

Now let's talk about the three stages in one method.

"Self-Improvement" is the beginning of the stage of "Entering into Calmness," "Gathering" is also "Self-Improvement," and "Hibernation" is also "Self-Improvement."

Thus, "Self-Improvement" is "Gathering" and "Hibernation."

The middle stage can be deduced by analogy.

You do not need to change the place of concentration, it will change by itself.

This is a formless orifice where all places are one place.

You do not need to change the times, but times will change by themselves.

It is called "Times without periods" - the moment of the original assemble-meeting of the world cycle.

If the heart-mind is not in a state of deep Calmness and Stillness, it cannot act.

The action caused by impulse is an accidental action, not a true action.

Therefore, it is said that an action that is influenced by things is human desire, and an action that is not influenced by things is the action of Heaven.

If you use things, then it is just the nature of human desire; if you do not use things on your own initiative, then it is the action of Heaven.

The action of Heaven is not opposed to the Original Nature - Xing of Heaven.

Now I want to explain the word "desire."

The essence of desire lies in the having of things.

Then thoughts are distorted and abnormal because actions are motivated (by the limited mind).

When not a single thought arises, then the right mindfulness is born, which is True Intention.

In the state of Profound Quietness of the Great Calmness, the Mechanism of Heaven is suddenly activated.

Is this not activation without thought?

Doing (Wéi) through Non-Doing (Wú Wéi), that is what it is.

The first sentence of this chapter has already fully summarized the role/function of the Golden Flower.

The second sentence of this chapter refers to the idea of the interconnection of the sun and moon, where "in the summer" refers to Fire, and "flying white snow" refers to the True Yin (line) in the middle of the Li-Fire trigram, which will be turned into the Kun-Earth trigram.

"Midnight" refers to the Kan-Water trigram, and "red sun" refers to the Yang line in the middle of the Kan-Water trigram, which will be turned into the Qian-Heaven trigram.

This is called "Taking from Kan-Water to fill in the Li-Fire."

The third sentence of this chapter explains the role/function of the handle of the Big Dipper, the whole mechanism of elevation and subsidence; does not "the water" refer to the Kan-Water trigram?

"Gentle wind" refers to the eyes; the shining of the eyes illuminates the Palace of Kan-Water and attracts the essence* of the Great Yang/Sun**.

* Here, it means the line of Yang inside the Kan-Water trigram.

** 太阳 (tài yáng) can be translated as Great Yang and also means the Sun. Thus, this explains why sunlight is considered to be pure Yang Qi energy.

"In heaven" refers to the Palace of Qian-Heaven trigram, and "floating and returning to feeding on the Virtue of Earth" is the "Spirit-Shen penetrates inside the Qi-Energy*" and "Heaven penetrates inside the Earth"; which is the process of the maintaining/ supporting the Fire.

* At the same time, you have to keep your True Intention for comprehending the Original Sense of the Reality that you have penetrated. You should always intend to penetrate to a more subtle reality, recognize and comprehend it. Never think that the work is already done and you have comprehended it all, when you start thinking like that, you will be caught in the Great Illusion.

The fourth sentence of this chapter points to the "secret within the secret," and "the secret within the secret" cannot be separated from the saying, "Washing the heart-mind and Cleansing from worries is Bathing."

The Teaching of Confucius starts with knowing how to establish yourself in the highest good; it begins with the Limitless - Wú Jí and returns to the Limitless - Wú Jí.

In Buddhism, there is a principle "The heart-mind does not have a permanent place/does not stay on any thing"*, which is the main idea of the Grand Canon**.

* This principle is taken from Jīn Gāng Jīng (金刚经), also known as the Diamond Sutra.

** Grand Canon is the collection of all Buddhist scriptures.

In Daoism, we use "Reaching the ultimate emptiness***" to complete all the work on the Original Nature - Xing and Vitality-Ming.

*** This principle is taken from Chapter 16 of Dao De Jing by Lao Zi.

Therefore, the Three Teachings do not go beyond these sayings, which are the Spiritual Elixir for overcoming death and gaining life.

What does Spiritual Elixir mean?

It means to be without (limited) the heart-mind in all situations.

Although, the most mysterious thing in our Daoist Teaching is Bathing.

However, the whole (Bathing) practice can be described in just two words "Emptiness of the heart-mind."

I used this simple sentence to uncover the mystery, saving you decades of investigation effort.

If you still do not understand the saying "three stages in one method," I will use the analogy of Buddhist Teaching: Emptiness, Conditional, Center.

Among these three views, the first one is "Emptiness," which means you should see all things as Empty*.

---

* "See all things as Empty" means that their essence is empty, they came from Nothingness and will be returned to Nothingness.

Therefore, their existence is temporary, and because of their temporary existence, they belong to the Emptiness.

"Conditional" means that although you know that all things are Empty, you still cannot destroy them, but build an appropriate attitude towards the circumstances, despite the fact that you are still in the Emptiness.

When you can neither destroy things nor attach to them, it is "Observing of the Center."

When you Cultivate the "Observing of the Center," you know that you cannot destroy things, but you also cannot attach to them, which means you are performing the Three Observations.

Since you are able to see the Emptiness, then while Cultivating the "Observing of the Emptiness," "Emptiness" is also Empty; "Conditional" is also "Observing of the Emptiness," and "Center" is "Observing of the Emptiness" too.

When you Cultivate the "Observing of the Conditional," mainly when using (things), then "Observing of the Conditional" is Conditional,

Emptiness is also Conditional, and Center is Conditional too.

Same approach with "Center," you are still "Observing of the Emptiness" in all things, but you don't call it "Emptiness," but call it "Center."

Also, practicing "Observing of the Conditional," you don't call it "Conditional," but call it "Center."

As for the "Center," you simply call it "Center."

Although sometimes I only speak of the Li-Fire trigram, sometimes I also talk of the Kan-Water trigram, but the main meaning has not changed in the end.

Opening my mouth, I say: "The essential mechanism is all in the two eyes."

"The essential mechanism" is about the usage/ function. If you know how to use it, you can control/ manage creation/transformations, but it would be wrong to say that creation/transformation is only about that.

Six Roots a Seven Orifices* are the storage of the Light.

* The Six Roots are eyes, ears, nose, tongue, body, and mind. The Seven Orifices are orifices of the eyes, ears, mouth, and nose.

So how could we take only two eyes and not deal with the rest?

You should use the Yang (line) of the Kan-Water trigram and the Light of the Li-Fire trigram for illumination, then you can achieve clarification/understanding.

Teacher Zhuzi once said: "It is not easy for a blind person to follow Daoist Cultivation, but it is not a problem for a deaf person.***"**

** Zhuzi, also known as Zhu Xi (1130-1200), also known as Master Zhu 朱子 (Zhū zǐ). He lived during the Song dynasty and was a Confucian writer and follower who is also considered the founder of Neo-Confucianism.

*** Despite the fact that the eyes are important for practicing Returning the Light, as has been mentioned many times in this text, but according to the Léng Yánjīng (楞严经 - "Surangama Sutra"), the inner hearing will allow you to achieve deeper penetration.

In general, it means that you can use any of your senses to practice this method.

How does that differ from what I said?

I'm just emphasizing who is the master and who is the assistant, what is less important and what is more important.

The sun and the moon are initially one thing.

The darkness in the sun is the Essence of the True Moon; the "Moon Cave" is not on the moon but on the sun.

That is why it is called the "Moon Cave", otherwise it would simply be called "moon".

The whiteness of the moon is the Light of the True Sun.

Sunlight reflected from the moon is called the "Root of Heaven," otherwise it would simply be called "heaven."

The Sun (without the Moon) and the Moon (without the Sun) are only half, but they form a whole body-substance when they unite.

It is like a single man or a single woman who cannot start a family while living alone, but when they become husband and wife, they can create a family.

However, using things as a metaphor in Daoist Cultivation is not entirely appropriate.

When husband and wife are separated, they are two persons; when the sun and moon are separated, they do not form a whole body-substance.

Once you understand this, you will understand that the eyes and ears are also a single whole.

I said that the blind person has no ears/hearing, and the deaf person has no eyes/sight.

From this point of view, what is one thing?

Two eyes?

Six Roots?

Six Roots are actually one root.

Seven Orifices?

Seven Orifices are actually one orifice.

What I am saying is just to show the similarities between them, so I do not see the duality.

Since you see them separately, then the separation has taken hold of your eyes.

Chapter 9

One Hundred Days

of

Building the Foundation

Xīnyìn Jīng* says: "The returning wind mixes and the work of one hundred days are spiritual**."

* This text has already been mentioned in Chapter 1, and my commentary is there.

** "Wind" refers to breathing, and "returning wind mixes" is the internal rotation and regulation of the Three Treasures through breathing. Pre-Celestial Three Treasures (Essens-Jing, Qi-Energy, Spirit-Shen) should be used for creating the Elixir, and before that, you have to regulate breathing. According to the text, it can be created in a hundred days, but you should not be tied to this period because it usually takes a much longer time. It all depends on your natural ability, the effort you put into practice, the duration of your Cultivation, and so on.

Also, pay attention to the word "spiritual," which means that you have to make your work spiritual. You should Cultivate Virtue-De, Cleanse your heart-mind of delusion and ignorance, have the True Intention for comprehending the Original Sence of the Primordial Realty and so on. That is what many students miss, they practice Ming Gong but ignore Xing Gong, but without Xing Gong your work will not be Spiritual.

Therefore, you can build the foundation in a hundred days, only then can you have the True Light.

Even if you work with the light of the eyes, it is not the Spiritual Fire, not the Light of the Original Nature, not the torch of Initial Wisdom.

Practicing the "Returning" in a hundred days, then Essens-Jing and Qi-Energy will naturally suffice.

True Yang arises spontaneously, and True Fire appears in Water.

If you keep following this way, then you will naturally achieve intercourse and form the embryo.

Thus, in the state of "unconsciously and unknowingly," the infant will be born*.

* You can find more information about these steps in Book 7.

If you still have a thought (in order to speed up these processes somehow), then you have left the Dao-Way.

A hundred days of building the foundation is not an actual hundred days; one day of building the foundation is not an actual one day.

One breath of building the foundation is not actual breathing.

The word "breath" consists of two characters "self/ from" and "heart-mind*."

* It was explained at the beginning of Chapter 4.

"Self/from" and "heart-mind" are the breathing of the Original Spirit-Shen, the Original Qi-Energy, and the Original Essens-Jing.**

** It can be read as "From the True Heart-Mind."

Ascent and descent, separation and unity proceed from the (True) Heart-Mind.

Being and Non-Being, Emptiness and Fullness rely/ depend on thought.

Breath is held for life, far more than a hundred days; therefore, a hundred days is just a part of the breath.

One hundred days is just a matter of empowerment.

During the day, you gain power, and at night you use it; at night, you gain power, and during the day, you use it.

A hundred days of building the foundation is a precious purpose.

All sayings of the True Immortals relate to the human body.

All sayings of the True Teachers relate to the disciples.

This is Mysterious within Mysterious, and it cannot be explained.

Only if you see the Original Nature - Xing then you will know.

Therefore, the student should seek a True Teacher; even if his Original Nature - Xing manifests itself in something, it will be beneficial for the student.

Chapter 10

The Light of Original Nature - Xing

and

the Light of Consciousness

The method of Returning the Light can be practiced whether you are walking, standing, sitting or lying down, but you have to find the key to this mechanism by yourself.

I already mentioned the state: "Light appears in the empty room," is not that light white?

But there is a thing that I want to remind everyone: when you start to practice, there is no light, but suddenly you see the light, that is the effect of practice.

But if the Light appears due to your work of thought/intentionally, you fall into the realm of consciousness and not the Light of Original Nature.

Therefore, you should not care whether you have light or not, so long as there are states of "No thought" and "Arising thought."

What is "No thought"?

It is like the saying: "With Thousands of cultivation methods (which are based on thoughts), you can reach a thousand places*."

What is "Arising thought?"

It is like the saying: "One thought can hold one life."

It indicates the place where the thought arises**, which is correct mindfulness***, and is not the same as ordinary thoughts.

** Means the state before the thought was born.

*** 正念 (zhèng niàn), or correct mindfulness, is the seventh step of the Noble Eightfold Path of Buddhism. These eight steps are Right View (正見), Right Inclinations (正思惟), Right Speech (正言), Right Conduct (正業), Right Livelihood (正命), Right Effort (正精進), Right Mindfulness (正念), Right Samadhi (正定).

The word "mindfulness" has two characters "now" and "heart-mind.***"

*** 念 means "mindfulness," where the upper part is 今 (jīn) means "now, present," and the lower part is 心 (xīn) means "heart-mind."

Therefore, "the present heart-mind" is mindfulness.

This heart-mind is also the Light and the Medicine.

Ordinary people just look at external things, but if you can see them as a reflection without discriminating*, then it is the Light of Original Nature - Xing.

* It does not mean that you cannot recognize one thing from another, but you can see that there is no essential difference between them, you see their essence, their true nature.

It is like a mirror or still water reflecting things unintentionally.

But when you start to see their differences, it becomes the Light of Consciousness.

It is like when there is already an image* in a mirror or still water, there is no more mirroring.

* In the sense that if an image gets stuck in the mirror due to its attachment to that image, then there will be no correct reflection of other things.

When there is consciousness in the Light, what kind of Light could it be?

When you return to the initial point, then it is the Light of Original Nature - Xing; when you have any thoughts, then it is the Light of Consciousness.

Once consciousness arises, the Light (of Original Nature - Xing) will disappear without a trace, and there is no way to find it.

Not that there was no Light at all, but that Light was transformed by consciousness.

This is what the Yellow Emperor's saying means: "Sound does not produce sound, but produces an echo**."

** Quoted from Liè Zǐ (列子) circa 450-375 BC, chapter 天瑞 (tiān ruì) "Omens of Heaven." The whole saying is "形动不生形而生影，声动不生声而生响，无动不生无而生有," which means "Form does not produce form but produces a shadow, sound does not produce sound but produces an echo, Non-Being does not produce Non-Being but produces Being."

In the introduction to the Léng Yán Jīng (Śūraṅgama Sūtra) says, "It is not in the dust/world of mortals, not in the consciousness, but only in the root/source."

What does this mean?

Dust/world of mortals is all external things, the worlds in which all beings can live.

It has nothing to do with your true self.

If you chase things, you are mistaking things for yourself.

Things have characteristics and features (and they must be returned to things).

Ventilation is a feature of doors and windows, brightness/light is a property of the sun and moon, but if you borrow it from them, you will eventually find that it is not really you/yours.

According to this, if there is a feature that still needs to be returned, if this thing is not you/yours, but whose is it?

You should return the brightness to the sun and moon, but since you have already seen the brightness of the sun and moon, it cannot be returned completely*.

* "It cannot be returned completely" because you already have discrimination/separation, and you are already in a world of duality. To bring it back completely, you must forget/get rid of any distinction/separation and return to non-duality.

Sometimes there is no sun or moon in the sky, but people always perceive the properties (of the sun and moon).

If so, can it be considered as your property that thing which distinguishes the sun and the moon?

Don't you know that discrimination is based on light and dark?

If light and darkness are forgotten, then where is the difference?

114

That is why it needs to be returned because it is internal dust.

Only the Seeing/Comprehension of the Original Nature - Xing** cannot be returned.

Here, the word "See" is not literally "see", otherwise it could be returned.

** The phrase "Seeing/Comprehension of the Original Nature - Xing" consists of only two characters 见性 (jiàn xìng), where the first character 见 translates as "see, observe, behold, perceive" and the second 性 translates as "nature, essence, quality." But if you put them together, you will get the special term, which means "Comprehension of the Original Nature."

If there is something to return, it means that you are still following conscious thoughts, then your Original Nature - Xing within the cycle of life and death/ Samsara.

This is similar to what Buddha says to Ananda: "If you are in the cycle of life and death/Samsara, you should blame your (limited) heart-mind and eyes*."

* This is a quote from Léng Yán Jīng (楞严经 - Śūraṅgama Sūtra).

When you start your Cultivation, there are seven perceptions/consciousness for recognizing things, and all of them must be returned one by one.

But when it comes to the eighth perception/ consciousness, let's temporarily leave aside "Comprehension of the Original Nature - Xing" and use the eighth perception/consciousness as the stick of Ananda**.

** Just as the stick helped Ananda walk, we can use the eight perception/consciousness to achieve the return to the source. That is the reason why we should be cleansed not only of the delusions that we know about but also of those that are hidden deep in our mind, and we are not even aware of them. You can find more information about this process in Book 10.

But as long as Original Nature - Xing contains all eight perceptions/consciousness***, it cannot be returned to the source.

*** The "eight perceptions/consciousness" (八识 - bāshí) is a Buddhist term.

The eight perceptions/consciousness are (1) 眼识 - perceptions of eyes, (2) 耳识 - perceptions of ears, (3) 鼻识 - perceptions of the nose, (4) 舌识 - perceptions of the tongue, (5) 身识 - perceptions of the body/touch, (6) 意识 - mind/thought perception, (7) 末那识 - Mònà consciousness, and (8) 阿赖耶识 - Alaya consciousness.

The first five are easy to understand, let's take a look at the next three.

"Mind/thought perception" is the perception with all five senses, on the basis of which judgments are made about the external world.

"Mònà consciousness" is the perception of your inner world that corresponds to self-awareness and self-attachment.

"Alaya consciousness" is a storage of karma seeds created in this and previous lives that will affect you in your next life.

Only if you eradicate it, then can you Comprehend the True Original Nature - Xing, which is truly undivided.

When you practice Returning the Light, you are returning the Original Undivided Light, so there is no need to use even a tiny piece of conscious thought.

The Six Roots are the cause of being in the cycle of life and death/Samsara, but when they are properly used,

Six Roots are also the cause of achieving enlightenment.

It is not about using the manifestations of the Six Roots when they have already reached and recognized things (and in a state of duality), but about using qualities/attributes within your Roots (when they are not manifested yet).

If you do not want to fall into (limited) consciousness, then during Returning the Light, you must use the Original Nature of the Six Roots.

If you have fallen into (limited) consciousness and are performing the Returning the Light, then you are using the consciousness nature of the Six Roots.

This is the subtle difference.

If you use the heart-mind, then it is the Light of Consciousness; but if you let go of the heart-mind, then it is the Light of Original Nature - Xing.

Although the difference is small, a mistake will take you a thousand miles astray, which is why you have to be discerning.

If the consciousness is not stopped, then the Spirit-Shen does not appear.

If the heart-mind is not emptied, then Elixir cannot be created.

If the heart-mind is cleansed, then you can get the Elixir.

If the heart-mind is emptied, then you can get the Medicine.

If you do not attach to any thing, then the heart-mind is clean.

If you do not desiderate any thing, then the heart-mind is empty.

If you see emptiness as emptiness, then it is not yet empty, but when you reach the state of "Forgetting that emptiness is empty," then it is True Emptiness.

Chapter 11

Merging of

Kan-Water and Li-Fire

When physical and mental power leaks and interacts with things, it is Li-Fire.

When you collect anything back with spirit or consciousness and keep it still and calm inside, it is Kan-Water.

When the Seven Orifices manifest themself and come out, it is Li-Fire.

When the Seven Orifices are turned inward, it is Kan-Water.

The Yin line (inside the Li-Fire trigram) follows the senses.

The Yang line (inside the Kan-Water trigram) brings the senses back.

Kan-Water and Li-Fire are Yin and Yang.

Yin and Yang are Original Nature - Xing and Vitality-Ming.

Original Nature - Xing and Vitality-Ming are body and heart-mind.

Body and heart-mind are Spirit and Radiance/Energy.

When your breath fades*, your physical and mental power will no longer interact with things and you will not be in the cycle of life and death/Samsara.

This is the True Merging.

Not to mention when you are immersed in silence with your legs crossed**.

* It means that in the state of deep meditation with True Intention, Kan-Water and Li-Fire can be merged. When they merge, the Great Elixir is formed, and you no longer belong to Samsara.

** Meditating in a cross-legged position will speed up your Cultivation and all transformations during it.

Chapter 12

The Cycle of Heaven

The Cycle of Heaven does not take Qi-Energy as the main thing, but the understanding of the heart-mind as a marvelous secret*.

*It indicates that feeling Qi-Energy is not the main goal of the practice. Feeling Qi is not a purpose of the practice, it is a necessary condition for successful practice. Do not confuse a condition with a goal. When you begin to feel Qi during Cultivation, it means that your work has just begun. The next step is you should shift your heart-mind to perceive more subtle things, to perceive a more subtle reality. You should use your True Intention, which you form with your heart-mind to achieve the state "Without heart-mind," to comprehend Qi, its Original Source...

If you want to ask how to implement the Cycle of Heaven, it is like "trying to help the shoots grow by pulling them upward"**.

** The characters used in the original text are 是助长也, where 是 means "is, are," 助长 means "encourage, foster, facilitate, help," and 也 is a classical final particle used in the classical language at the end of a sentence or clause. Because of the meaning of the first character, the next two simply represent part of the idiom 揠苗助长, which means "trying to help the shoots grow by pulling them upward."

The only thing you need to do is to guard the state of "Without heart-mind" and follow "Without thought."

Look at the sky, it changes constantly, all 365 days, but the North Star never moves, and neither does my heart-mind.

Heart-mind is like the North Star, and Qi-Energy is like all other stars.

Qi-Energy in our body passes through all the limbs and bones, so do not use too much force (during any work with Qi).

At first, refine-cleanse your Conscious Spirit, eliminate ignorance and delusions, then the Medicine can appear.

The Medicine is not a material thing, but the Light of Original Nature - Xing.

It is the Pre-Celestial True Qi-Energy, but you have to be in a state of Great Stillness and Calmness, only then can you notice it.

There is no other way to collect it, and anyone who says that there is another way to collect it is deeply mistaken.

After a long time (of being in a state of Great Stillness and Calmness), the best features of the heart-mind become radiant and clear.

Then the heart-mind naturally becomes empty and you are freed from the cycle of life and death/ Samsara; you achieve liberation from rebirth and the ocean of dust/mundane world.

If today you (only) talk about "dragon and tiger" and tomorrow about "water and fire" (but don't even try to practice and implement it), then, in the end, it will become just delusions.

I received this method from True Person Huǒlóng* and do not know what other elixir books say.

* Huǒlóng (火龙) literally means "Fiery Dragon."

Each day has a Cycle of Heaven and each hour has a Cycle of Heaven.

When Kan-Water and Li-Fire interact, it is also a Cycle.

When I merge them into my body, it is the Cycle-Rotation** of Heaven.

You should not stop it (merging); (you should also understand that there is) time of interaction and time without interaction (and both of them are important).

But the Cycle-Rotation of Heaven never stops.

If you achieve the fusion of Yin and Yang, spring will come to the whole Earth*.

* This is an allegory of the fact that in spring, everything is awake and filled with energy.

In the properly established Central Palace, all things naturally grow and flourish, which is called "Bathing" in the elixir books.

What is that if it's not the Great Cycle of Heaven?

These are the Fire Times-Periods, and although they can be small or great, in reality, there is no difference between them.

When you are proficient in this art and it becomes natural, you will no longer see the difference between such things as Kan-Water and Li-Fire, Heaven and Earth.

Who does the interaction, who makes it one Cycle or two Cycles, or where to find the difference between great and small?

In short, this is the rotation/operation/function in the body, although it appears to be something extremely large or small.

When there is a rotation-circulation, then Heaven, Earth and all things rotate-circulate with it.

Although this happens in a square inch (i.e., in a small place/space), it is also extremely large.

Fire Times-Periods of the Golden Elixir should be natural/spontaneous.

When it is not natural/not spontaneous, then Heaven and Earth remain (ordinary) Heaven and Earth, all things remain (ordinary) things.

If you try to force them to unite, you won't be able to do this.

For instance, if there is a severe drought*, then Yin and Yang will not merge, Qián-Heaven and Kūn-Earth will not rotate during the day (as they should), and eventually, you will see many unnatural things.

* Indicates extreme and lack of balance and harmony.

If you can rotate Yin and Yang and regulate them naturally, then suddenly the sky will become cloudy and it will rain.

Plants and trees will be watered, and mountains and rivers will flow freely.

At this time, even if something is wrong, it will quickly disappear when you notice it.

This is called the Great Cycle of Heaven.

Someone asked: Is the Living** Zi time (midnight) wonderful and subtle?

** It is called "living" because the Yang is born and starts growing at that time period.

First, you need to recognize the Correct Zi time, which is not an actual midnight.

If it is not the actual midnight and you cannot point to the Correct Zi time, then how can you recognize the Living Zi time?

When you know the Living Zi time, there is also the Correct Zi time.

They are one and two, neither Correct (Zi time) nor Living (Zi time); if you are able to see their real essence, then you will see that there is nothing not Correct and there is nothing not Living.

If you cannot see the truth/real essence, can you figure out which one is Living and which one is Correct?

As for the Living Zi time, you should be able to see it all the time, then you will succeed.

When you reach the Correct Zi time, your aspiration/will become clear and bright, and the Living Zi time will appear.

If you still cannot recognize the Living Zi time, then you should temporarily remain in the Correct Zi time;

when the Correct Zi time is understood, the Living Zi time will also manifest its spiritual miraculousness.

Chapter 13

Song of

Inspiration for

All People

I am leaving the world, but because of the warmth of my cinnabar heart* to the liberation of the world, I do not skimp on warmhearted** advice and inspiring words and I do this in abundance.

* It is an allegory that means "a heart full of compassion."

**The characters used in the original text are 婆心 which means "kindheartedness, a kind and compassionate heart." But they are also part of the idiom 苦口婆心, which means "advice in earnest words and with good intention, exhort with sincere words prompted by a kind heart, speak earnestly and patiently and with the best intention."

Buddha also pointed out the chain of cause and effect, which are the reason for life and death, and this is indeed a pity (that many people overlook this).

Lao Jun also talked about suffering from having a body and "self/I" and transmitted the Teaching of the Spirit-Shen of Valley, but people did not recognize and did not appreciate it.

Now I am talking about finding the True Path:

The Yi Jing/Book of Changes says***: "Yellow Center**** is the (key) for comprehension of the

highest principle of all things," and "The right state" is the Mysterious Gate.

*** The full quote from Yi Jing is "君子黄中通理，正位居体，美在其中而畅于四支，发于事业，美之至也," which means "The noble person uses the Yellow Center for comprehension of the highest principle of all things, remaining in the right state; there is a beauty/goodness inside of it and it freely reaches and fills the four limbs (whole body), extends throughout all your activities, and this is highest beauty/goodness."

**** "Yellow Center" (黄中) has several meanings. According to Wu Xing (Five Phases), yellow is the color of the Earth, which is located in the center and indicates the True Intention we should have in order to comprehend True Reality. It also signifies the heart and internal/hidden De-Virtue.

During Zi time (midnight), Wu time (noon), and in between, your breathing should be stabilized and calm, then the Light returns to the ancestor's orifice and all spirits* calm down.

* "All spirits" is a term that comes from the religious beliefs of Daoism, according to which each desire has its own spirit-master. Therefore the

phrase "all spirits calm down" simply means that all your thoughts and desires are calm.

The One Qi-Energy appears from the Source that produces the Medicine and penetrates through the screen/curtain, transforming into the Golden Light.

The red sun always shines and people mistake it for the Essence of Kan-Water and Li-Fire.

They try to move/shift the heart and kidneys but only succeed in their isolation; then how can the way of people be in balance and harmony with the Heart-Mind of Heaven?

If the way is in balance and harmony with Heaven, they (Kan-Water and Li-Fire) will meet naturally.

Drop aside all interconnections (causes and effects) of all phenomena, then not even a single thought can arise.

This is the True Limitless-Wu Ji of the Pre-Celestial, the Great Emptiness is profound and unmanifested.

Original Nature - Xing and Vitality-Ming is the key to the state of Forgetfulness of conscious thoughts / mind-thought perception.

When the state of Forgetfulness of conscious thoughts / mind-thought perception is achieved, then you can see the True Source.

The water is clear/calm and the pearl appears, it is mysterious and incomprehensible; all beginningless delusion and suffering are eliminated at once.

From the Heaven of Jade Purity,* the Register/List accompanied by the Nine Dragons has been descended; now you can step on the cloud and ascend to the Gate of Heaven; you can control the wind and lightning to create thunder.

* See commentary in chapter 8.

Condensation/coagulation of Spirit-Shen and calm breathing is a starting point/mechanism, retreat to a hidden place** to achieve total solitary and tranquility.

** The reason for this action is described in "Book 10 - Retreat Program."

Earlier, I pointed out the correct path for Zhang Zhennu with two poems* for her about the Great Dao-Way.

* The first poem is: "道无巧妙，与你方儿一个。子后午前定息坐，夹脊双关昆仑过。想时得气力，思量我," which means "Dao-Way is artless and unsophisticated, and I give you the next instruction. After midnight and before noon, sit and calm your breath, and (you will feel how the Qi-Energy) passes through the double pass of Jiājí^ into Kunlun,^^ gaining the power of Qi and contemplating yourself".

And the second one: "坎离坤兑分子午，须认自家宗祖。地雷震动山头雨，要洗濯黄芽出土。捉得金精牢闭固，辩甲庚，要生龙虎。待他问汝甚人传，但说先生姓吕," which means "Kan-Water and Li-Fire, Kun-Earth and Dui-Lake^^^ are part of Zi time (midnight) and Wu time (noon) and you must recognize your own ancestors. When the Earth shakes and Thunder rumbles - it rains in the mountains; after the water leaves, magnificent Yellow Sprouts emerge from the earth. Grab the Essence of Metal^^^^ and lock it tight. Recognize and Cultivate Jiǎ and Gēng^^^^^, and the Dragon and Tiger will be born. If you ask who pass me this teaching, I will answer: Venerable Teacher Lǚ (Dongbin)."

^ *Jiaji is one of the three Gates on your spine. There are Three Gates (三关 - sān guān) on the Governing Vessel (Du Mai) through which Qi passes during circulation in the Small Heaven Circle (小周天 - xiǎo zhōu tiān). The Three Gates are Wei Lu (尾闾关), Jiaji (夾脊关) and Yuzhen (玉枕关). Wei Lu is the tailbone, Jiaji is the middle of the upper back between the two*

137

shoulder blades, Yuzhen or Jade Pillow is the base of the skull or occipital area.

^^ Kunlun is a name for the Kunlun Mountain range; in the human body, it symbolizes the crown of the head.

^^^ These are all trigram names.

^^^^ 金精 (Jīn jǐng) can be translated as the Essence of Metal, as well as the Golden Essence. I chose "The Essence of Metal" because of its context and similarity to analogies to the text by Zhang Boduan's (张伯端) "Wu Zhen Pian" (悟真篇 - "Chapters on Awakening to True Reality").

^^^^^ The 1st and 7th heavenly stems, which according to Wu Xing are Wood and Metal.

"After midnight and before noon" is not about times, but Kan-Water and Li-Fire.

"Calm your breath" means that with each breath, you should return to the root-source, which is also "The Yellow Center."

"Sit" means that the heart-mind does not move.

"Jiājí" is not only about the place on the spine but also about the Great Path right to the Jade Capital*.

"Double pass" is hard to explain in words.

"When the Earth shakes and Thunder rumbles - it rains in the mountains" is about the emergence of the True Qi-Energy.

"Yellow Sprouts emerge from the earth" means that the Medicine is born.

These two short poems completely explain the Great Path of Cultivation.

They are clear and if you understand them, then you will not be confused by other people's random theories.

Once, Confucius and Yan Hui climbed to the top of Mount Tai and saw a white horse galloping at the foot of the mountain on the border of the southern state.

Yan Hui said: "Seeing the path of a running white horse looks like a piece of white cloth."

Confucius covered Yan Hui's eyes with his hand.

He (Yan Hui) was wasting too much of his vision power.

As a result, the Light of the Spirit-Shen is gone, which is why you need to follow the method of Returning the Light.

Returning the Light should be practiced with a pure heart-mind, you only need to condense your True breath in the Central Palace, and after a long time the natural spiritual transformations will occur.

It is based on the state of Calmness and Stillness of the heart-mind.

Forgetting/Forgetfulness the heart-mind and condensing the Qi-Energy is the result of Cultivation.

When Qi-Energy is calm and the heart-mind is empty, then the Elixir can be formed.

When the heart-mind and Qi-Energy unite, it is soft/warm Cultivation.

When you comprehend the Original Nature - Xing, it is Dao-Way.

All of you should practice hard because even a small mistake can cause the Light to disappear, and it will be a pity.

If you miss one day of Cultivation, then that day you are a kind of ghost.

If you can (Returning the Light) with each breath, then you can become the True Immortal during that breath.

You should work hard on this.

Daoist Cultivation, Book 1: Fundamental Theory and Philosophy: Explanation of Qigong, Neigong and Neidan

Daoist Cultivation, Book 1 has detailed explanations of Fundamental Daoist Theory and Philosophy. Basic terms such as Qigong, Neigong, Neidan, Jing-Qi-Shen, Wu Xing, Ming Gong, Xing Gong are explained in detail.

This book is recommended for everyone interested in Traditional Daoist methods of Self Development as well as for those who practice Qigong, Neigong, Neidan, or Taichi. The explanation of the theories of Yin-Yang and Wu-Xing is given with a traditional understanding, which explains the essential meaning that is omitted or misinterpreted in modern sources. The book describes the Three Ways of Self Development, where you will learn the main difference between religious Daoism and Spiritual Daoism. The chapter "Gate of all Marvelous-Mysterious" is devoted to a crucial state you should have during practice on the way to the Original state of comprehending Primordial. In addition, the book also has a chapter on "Centers and Channels," which is dedicated to explaining the nature of the Dantians and the Energy system with pictures and correlations of 12 standard meridians and Extraordinary channels.

"Building the Foundation," "Body Foundation," "Heart-Mind Foundation," "The Virtue Cultivation or where students should start" are other topics of the book.

Daoist Cultivation, Book 2: Cultivation of the Original Nature - Xing Gong: The essential work for Qigong, Neigong and Neidan

This book explains in detail the essential part of Daoist cultivation, the **Cultivation of the Original Nature** (Xing Gong).

You can find fundamental methods such as **Virtue Cultivation, Purification of the mind and heart from impurities, Dissolving ignorance.** In the Chapter "**Obstacles and Distractions,**" you'll find their description and ways to avoid them.

It is backed up by translations of Daoist texts such masters as **Wang Chongyang, Zhang San Feng,** etc.

In addition to those mentioned above, two translated texts, "**Lao Jun exalts one hundred medicine**" and "**Lao Jun speaks about one hundred diseases.**"

Daoist Cultivation, Book 3: Ming Gong: Qigong, Neigong and Neidan: 1st Level of Inner Alchemy + Video

You will find a detailed description of Qigong/Neigong methods for Inner Alchemy (Neidan): "Gathering Qi of Heaven and Nature," "Daoist Breathing Techniques," "Zhan Zhuang," and many others.

As well as a description of essential practices of the first level of Inner Alchemy such as "Stabilize Furnace and Set Up Cauldron," "Collecting the Ingredients" and "Elixir Cultivation."

In addition to the Qigong and Neigong (Ming Gong) techniques, you will learn how the Cultivation of the Original Nature (Xing Gong) should be practiced during each of the Ming Gong methods. It is the most mysterious and almost unknown part of Daoist Inner Alchemy which will lead you to the awakening of your Primordial Wisdom.

The book includes instructional photos and even has a link to a Youtube video playlist. Thus you can be sure that you are doing exercises correctly.

Daoist Cultivation, Book 4: The Classic: 24 Essential Instructions for Disciples - Translation and Commentary

This book presents a translation of the Daoist text "24 essential instructions for disciples" written by Liu Yiming. As you may know, traditional texts are written in a very specific language and style and can be difficult for many readers to understand.

That is why the translation is accompanied by comments explaining the 24 instructions in a language that everyone understands.

How important is this text? Let's quote Liu Yiming:

"These twenty-four essential instructions mentioned above are crucial gates and key points that you must put into practice. You have to go through all of them, accept, understand, and realize each one; only then you will be able to meet the True Teacher and hear about the Great Dao. If there is even one instruction that you cannot realize and practice, even if you meet the True Teacher and hear about the Dao, the result will be unpredictable and may possibly lead nowhere."

Daoist Cultivation, Book 5: Elixir Cultivation: Qigong, Neigong and Neidan - Second Level + Video

This Book is the Second part of a practical guide to traditional Daoist Cultivation. You will find a traditional approach and explanation of the fundamental Ming Gong techniques.

The book contains a detailed description of Qigong/Neigong methods not only for health but also for Inner Alchemy (Neidan): "Dynamic Attunement to Nature," "Improving Qi Circulation in Arm Meridians," "Zhan Zhuang - second level," and others.

You will also continue to learn Elixir Cultivation: Middle Dantian Cultivation, Zhong Mai Cultivation, Zhong Mai and Two Dantians Cultivation.
Small Heavenly Circulation - the traditional method of Opening Du Mai and Ren Mai.

The book also includes a translation of the Daoist text "Wondrous Scripture for the daily internal practice of the Great Taishang Lao Jun".

The book includes instructional photos and even has a link to a Youtube video playlist. Thus you can be sure that you are doing exercises correctly.

If you have bought any paper book from our Daoist Cultivation series, you can get the same ebook for free from us. Just send us a photo of your order confirmation and book, and we will send you an e-book. You can find our Instagram and Facebook pages in the book.

Daoist Cultivation, Book 6: Chapters on Awakening to the True Reality: The Daoist Classic

Wu Zhen Pian (悟真篇), or Chapters on Awakening to the True Reality, is one of the most advanced and well-known treatises on Daoist Inner Alchemy. It was written by the Daoist Master Zhang Boduan (张伯端) around 1068-1077 and is addressed to students already familiar with the fundamental knowledge of Daoist practice and philosophy.
Although some of the verses may not be easy for beginners to understand, it is still worth studying this treatise because it will help you touch with the profound wisdom of the Daoist tradition.

The translation includes:
Foreword by Zhan Boduan
Upper Scroll - Sixteen chapters
Middle Scroll - Sixty-four chapters
Lower Scroll - One verse and Sixteen chapters
Five quatrains,
Afterword by Zhan Boduan.

Daoist Cultivation, Book 7: Alchemical Principles: Twenty-Four Secret Instructions for Disciples by Liu Yiming

This book presents the text *"Alchemical Principles: Twenty-Four Secret Instructions for Disciples" by Liu Yiming.*

This is quite a unique text that explains the various stages and highest principles of Daoist Inner Alchemy.
Moreover, this is not only a translation but also an accompanying commentary to each instruction and explaining each line of the text. The information in this book is pretty exceptional and recommended for every serious practitioner.

To quote what Liu Yiming said about this text: "These twenty-four secret instructions are a step-by-step description of the Fire Times-periods that should be studied and fully understood since the slightest deviation of one hair will lead to a huge mistake of thousands of miles." ... "Followers of the Dao-Way must clearly understand what these topics mean, know from beginning to end when to hurry and when to rest, and have a clear point of view. If something is not completely clear, then it is just a waste of time and effort."

Daoist Cultivation, Book 8: Dao De Jing by Lao Zi

Dao De Jing (道德經) is the most famous Daoist text in the world. According to history, it was written by Lao Zi (老子) about 2500-2300 years ago. I know that there are a lot of translations of this text, and some of you may fairly ask: Why do I need one more?

Once, I published on Facebook a piece of text from my Book 1 that talked about breathing techniques. One person in his comment wrote the next: "Dao de Jing, chapter 55, expressly warns against interfering with the breath". I told him that it was incorrect and that breathing techniques are part of Daoist Teaching. He replied, "Look at chapter 55 of Dao De Jing, Gia-fu Feng (Feng Jia-fu) translation". I checked that transaction and found the next line: "Controlling the breath causes strain." Then I opened the original text of Dao De Jing and saw that it didn't even have the word "breath" in it. The character Qi (氣) was translated as "breath," which is inaccurate in this case.

Moreover, the translated line, such as "Controlling the breath causes strain," stands out sharply against the background of other semantic sentences in chapter 55 that list benefits for a person. Thus translation was made incorrect.

The original line says 心使氣曰強 which should be read as "Using the mind-heart to control Qi is called being strong and powerful." As you can see, it has a totally another sense. I realized that despite the fact that there are more than a hundred translations only in English, many of them may contain misleading information. Of course, I didn't check them all, it is simply impossible, I just decided to translate it myself.

Daoist Cultivation, Book 9 - Collection: 15 Discourses by Wang Chongyang, Qingjing Jing, Yinfu Jing

This book is a collection of Daoist texts that every follower of the Teaching should know. These are: "Fifteen Discourses Establishing the Teaching by Wang Chongyang," "Qingjing Jing - Scripture on Clarity and Stillness," and "Huang Di Yinfu Jing - Scripture on Hidden Talismans by Emperor Huang Di."

"Fifteen Discourses Establishing the Teaching by Wang Chongyang" is not only translated but also provided with my commentary on them. I have tried to explain each "discourse" and every detail of the text. That is why I did only some footnotes to the translated "Qingjing Jing" and "Huang Di Yinfu Jing" texts, which were not explained in Wang Chongyang's treatise.

Qingjing Jing is one of the most important Daoist texts, along with Dao De Jing, but unfairly much less popular in the West. Even though it is much shorter than DDJ, it is incredibly deep and contains extremely profound wisdom.

There are two versions of Huangdi Yinfujing, a shorter text containing about 300+ characters and a longer text containing approximately 400+ characters, in three sections. The current translation presents the longer one.

Daoist Cultivation, Book 10 - Retreat Program: + Translation of Wang Chongyang's text

This book is about the Retreat Program. In the book, you can find the traditional recommendations for the retreat and answers to the following topics:

- How to choose the right place for a retreat?

- What should you know about the retreat?

- General Retreat Schedule

- How to deal with this program?

- Detailed Information about methods you should practice during the retreat.

A translation of the text "The True Man (Wang) Chongyang transmits (Ma) Danyang Twenty-Four Secrets" is added at the end of the book.

Daoist Cultivation, Book 11 - Zhang Sanfeng: The Daoist Classic - Translation and Commentary

This book presents texts by Daoist Master Zhang Sanfeng, such as **"Speaking of the Dao in Simple Words" and "Song of Meditation."**

Both translated texts are accompanied by commentaries in which I explain difficult-to-understand passages. The original text of "Speaking of the Dao in Simple Words" was written without chapters, but for convenience, I have broken it into some parts, given them titles, and put them in brackets. I did it because it has many topics and it was easy to get confused, and it's more clear now.

In addition to the translations, commentaries have been added to these texts.

Sometimes I explain the meaning of the terms, show the Chinese characters, and explain why I translated them one way or another.

The text "Song of Meditation" is not so large but dense in meaning.

These texts are highly recommended to everyone who is interested in studying Daoist Teaching.

If you would like to learn more about Daoism, you can follow my pages

Instagram https://www.instagram.com/taichi_losangeles

Facebook https://www.facebook.com/

DaoismTaichiLosAngeles

If you have questions or want me to clarify some details of Daoist philosophy or practice, you can send them via Facebook or Instagram.

If you have questions about group classes, private classes, online consultations, or workshops in your city, you can contact me via Instagram or Facebook page.

Daoist Cultivation Press

Los Angeles, CA, USA

Made in United States
North Haven, CT
31 October 2024